Psalms O

Subtitle: In The M

Answer

Dedicated to the memory of my father Merrick Zachary 2/5/53 to 5/4/87

Thanks for always believing in me to do more with my life and to share the heart that you have for the world and the compassion for the work to make sure everyone was taken care of. I will always love you for that period to my baby boy William Zachary downs thanks for pushing me to do greater with everything that I do with my gifts that the Lord has blessed me with. To share my life's work with you to know that you can do anything with your mind and become greater. Never allow anyone to dim your light for it will never stop shining. A life of poetry can hit you from all angles to help see through different eyes through a writer. These psalms will make you think, cry, smile and laugh, but most of all will make you see God in a new way.

A Mother Worth— 5/9/20

Psalms Of A Prophet

Subtitle: In The Midst of It All I got an Answer

Hidden in the depth of a cave was carved out the rarest of the finest rock,
having the ability to shine so bright like the hands on the clock.

To be able to capture the man's heart,
She will carry him, and her love will never depart.

She was tricked one time by the little snake,
but from that day forward she carried the power to discern the fake.

The Lord said she shall bruise the enemy's head,
She would give her last to make sure everyone is fed.

The way she walks by you without even having to say anything,
the fragrance she gives calls man to bring a ring.

When she feels down or hurt, she falls to her knees,
says to the father, "can you help me please?"

She will sacrifice her life for her loved ones,
Be careful how you handle her, she has the ability to carry tons.

She is not defined by what a man thinks,
She is worth more than silver or gold and her ship will never sink.

She possesses a power in that she will always bounce back,
Please treat her well, she will help you get back on track.

She is the heartbeat that will carry the family through,
She makes sure that the whole community knows what to do.

Psalms Of A Prophet

Subtitle: In The Midst of It All I got an Answer

A mother's worth is so precious that it mends the broken heart,
her love will last until the end, and it will never depart.

Handle her worth with pride,
for this mother's love will never leave your side.

A Place Called Yet

In this place I must speak to you,
A place of quietness to bring you through.

In this place there is pain there,
In the process your heavy load I will share.

In this place are lonely nights,
In these battles there will be fights.

In this place the winds blow hard,
Being a prisoner in mind where everything is barred.

In this place, life is created in you,
If you are able to stand and make it through.

A place called, "Yet", says what is next,
You must stay in the word and read my text.

In this place storms rises up,
But yet, I will fill your broken cup.

Psalms Of A Prophet

Subtitle: In The Midst of It All I got an Answer

In this place called, "Yet" there is a process to do,
To be remade, reborn just to make a brand new you.

In this place miracles birth out,
And you will realize that angels walk about.

In this place trouble water will flow,
But the walls in your life will come down with one blow.

In this place called yet you getting to know me,
So, you may experience life more abundantly.

In this the place you must trust me,
In this place called, "Yet" you can walk in liberty.

Because of Yet I have liberty,
Just because you worshipped me.

A Place

I hear a cry in the dark someone reaching out for help,
They can't seem to face what life has dealt.

They're wondering will this be the day when everything ends,
They are tired of being tossed around like leaves in the wind.

I feel their pain it's all they know,
The surroundings of disappointment brought them far below.

Here take my hand and I will lead you,
Don't be afraid, I know exactly what to do.

Psalms Of A Prophet

Subtitle: In The Midst of It All I got an Answer

It's up to you to follow me there,
A place called, "Peace" where everyone cares.

I know it's hard to believe that a place like that exist,
Believe me it took me awhile to get there but it truly exists.

The train is coming you can get aboard,
Doesn't even need a ticket just come to the blessing out pour?

Fear will drive you to place you don't want to be,
But peace will cause you to expect yourself to walk in integrity.

Take my hand, I will lead,
You don't have to fight, kill, not one plea,
Because Jesus paid it all on the cross at Calvary.

A Prayer Of Concern 2-24-11

Hello God, it's me down here seeking your face,

Psalms Of A Prophet

Subtitle: In The Midst of It All I got an Answer

I need a word with you I have a serious situation I need to plead this case.

There are some things in my life that I just don't understand, seems like everything is going down like a person stuck in quicksand.

My heart bleeds from all the pain and lies, the jealousy the back biting the ones who stab you in your side.

You are the God of all things made right, Somewhere something happened that all we do is fight, fight, fight!

You are the God of War and the God of peace, Can you answer me why your people act like beasts?

So, there is no justice among us, and we know nothing about right living, We see people in need, and they take, and we are giving.

When will love abound in our hearts? Can we do what is right, can we actually do our part?

They hatch deadly snakes and weave spider webs that whoever falls into the web would die, Where is love because something must be wrong with our eyes.

Psalms Of A Prophet

Subtitle: In The Midst of It All I got an Answer

You said never have I seen the righteous forsaken nor your
seed begging bread,
we must have missed it especially if we are feeding each other
's lead.

We walk like the blind along a wall feeling our way like people
without eyes,
We would rather turn our face from you and watch you die.

Father tears cannot stop flowing from all this pain,
It just seems like everyone has lost their mind and went insane.

Father, I decided that I would be the one to make a difference
in somebody's life,
Even if I die trying, I am willing to make the ultimate
sacrifice.

Breathe on me your power to stand,
never let me go please father hold my hand!

I am glad you said that you will never leave me nor forsake me
you will be with me until the end,
I hear you father who will go who can I send?

Here I am Lord send me,
equip me with your armor so that I can fulfill my destiny.

I see your hand reaching down with fire all around,

Psalms Of A Prophet

Subtitle: In The Midst of It All I got an Answer

my God I hear the trumpets blowing what a glorious sound.

What I don't have to fight alone I see your angels coming to stand by me,
oh Lord thank you I know I can fight with all your strategies.

Don't be ignorant of the devil's devices because he will attack,
but know that the Trinity has your back.

Trust and lean on your savior for he has you,
for the holy war has come but there is a victory for you.

I hear the angels encamped all around me,
I see them dancing in the fire for they got the victory!

For this is a prayer of concern this you see,
but I do believe that the battle is won, and we'll continue to get the blessings from thee.

Am I Not God?

Psalms Of A Prophet

Subtitle: In The Midst of It All I got an Answer

When you were crying, I heard you,

Didn't I say that I was going to carry you through?

It does matter how you may think the circumstances is going to turn out,

Let me be God the one that stands about.

I saw you when you got up to praise me in the middle of the night,

Did you think I would leave there in a dim light to fight?

Am I not God, the God that cares so much for you?

The same God that promises to see you through.

I look down from heaven and saw a wretch undone,

I chose you the work in your life that has begun.

Who do you think that I am an unfair God that lies?

Am I not the same God that helps you to survive?

I and only I Am the one to judge you,

Expect it any day I coming to bless you all the way through.

Worrying never solved the problem that you were face with in life,

Only I will not have you ignorant of Satan devices.

Psalms Of A Prophet

Subtitle: In The Midst of It All I got an Answer

I heard you say where are you now God when I need you,

Did I deny you or did I see you through?

The thoughts you have in the night and in the day, I heard them,

When your body was racking in pain, and you asked if I could just touch his hem.

My grace is sufficient meaning I gave you just enough to make it through,

Now you ask God what is for me to do.

Stand still and know that I Am God that's what I told you,

Did you listen, now you turn a deaf ear and now there are few.

You want to be an instrument for me, yet you are doing it your way,

How am I going to use you if you are moving without me today?

Am I not the same God that bless you in the pass and yet you doubt me?

Who am I a God that can't give you total victory?

I heard you when you said I can't go on anymore,

But when you did it yourself it did not work and now, you're faced with life's gore.

Am I not the same God that has giving you favor?

Psalms Of A Prophet

Subtitle: In The Midst of It All I got an Answer

And yet the harvest is great and there is little that labor.

I say to you if you don't trust me, when will you?

I am the same God over your life that blesses you through and through,

Let me be God I know what to do,

And that is to come by and serve you.

An Honorable Thought

To rise up is to stand,
To honor is to bow down with an open hand.

To be free is to walk in liberty,
To see your future is to walk in your destiny.

To prioritize is to read your word,
To talk to the Lord is to listen to what you heard.

Psalms Of A Prophet

Subtitle: In The Midst of It All I got an Answer

To see the impossible is to see your future,
To grow in the Lord is to embrace his nurture.

To be peculiar is to be set apart,
To have favor is to walk with God's heart.

To have the heart of God is to have the compassion for such a time,
To go through trials is to say nothing like a mime.

To be passionate about what you do,
Is to confront the demons that would try to bind you.

To be comfortable in a place where the enemy is on a rampage,
Would be like living like a bird in a nasty cage.

Call on the Lord while He may be found,
Persist, pursue while the love is all around.

Value the Lord and all that He do,
Just think about it, he created me and you.

For wolf has been set out to destroy all that he can,
But you see he forgot I was place in the master hand.

And Yet I'm Calling You

Psalms Of A Prophet

Subtitle: In The Midst of It All I got an Answer

In the middle of the day, I heard a still small voice calling,
Saying my child, you are falling.

Falling from my mercy and my grace,
Living life without love is as an empty place.

A place where there is no freedom to worship me,
And yet I am calling you to a place called peace.

I see your tears rolling down your face,
With your mind just wondering and wondering on empty space.

And yet I'm calling you to come out,
Calling you break forth in praise and shout.

Every wonder why you went through so much,
So, you can rise above your giants, so they can be crushed.

Push through those barriers that you have put up,
Let me guide you and seal that broken cup.

I've called you to be set aside for purpose in your life,
It was I the Son of God that made the ultimate sacrifice.

No more walking in the valley of the shadows of death,
See the mountain top and sore like wings on a jet.

Press forward and don't look back,
I'm holding you with my mighty hand, I won't let you fall off track.

Psalms Of A Prophet

Subtitle: In The Midst of It All I got an Answer

And yet I am calling you to go higher in me,
That's what I called you to do walk in your destiny.

Go forward; this is what you must do,
Not looking back, you must go through,
And realize God the Father have called you.

"And yet you deny me."

I was on the forefront of the battle looking for you,
But you stood in the background saying, "what do you want me to do"?

I look for you to help win this war,
But yet you chose something else to sit around the bar.

When they came to carry me away to die, I looked around for you and you were not there,
They ask if you knew me, and you act like you did not even care.

I went before the people and watch them put down my father you see,
I was wondering when they people approach you what you'd do and yet you deny me.

A tear drops from my face in shame that you turn your back on me,
After I told you, you would deny me 3x's and you said who not me.

I thought we were friends to the end,
But I see that you are not the one I can send.

Did you not know that I love you, that I want the best for thee?
And yet when the people came to you, you turn around and deny me.

I forgive you because you were scared to rise up,
But when it's all said and done, I will seal that broken cup.

Don't let fear have you to deny me,
Rise up and walk and fulfill your destiny.

Psalms Of A Prophet

Subtitle: In The Midst of It All I got an Answer

Don't you know every time you say that is not me?
You kill the plans that I see.

I see greater in you that will take you into a place I could not go,
Take charge of your destiny for this I know.

You will not fold and bow your head in shame of your past,
For remember the last shall be first, and the first shall be last.

Lift your head child and proclaim the word that is in your mouth,
Walk around the wall of Jericho and shout about.

For the glory of the Lord is upon you,
I've called you Holy, now you know what to do.

I have anointed you and my hand is upon you,
Cry loud to the people and whatever your hands find to do you do.

No more denying me for I have destroyed every dead thing for thee,
For you will never again deny me!

"Broken and Yet He Loves Me"

Broken and in despair yet we fight on to see the end,
Wonder what to do, where to go, or who can we send.

Broken and in despair yet we fight on to see the end,
We strive to make it, to be talked about and yet do we offend?

I'm crying, I don't understand who I am anymore!
Instead, I'm confronted with life's unmerciful gore.

Psalms Of A Prophet

Subtitle: In The Midst of It All I got an Answer

Down and out, who is there to turn to?
There's a knock at the door, who is it trying to come through?

I've closed that door so many times before,
But someone is persistent to walk in that closed door.

I'm afraid that hurt will come again if I let them in,
But a whisper in my ear said, "you my child will win".

I did not understand why me? I am undeserving of such victory,
But that whisper came again saying because you mean so much to me,
I laid my life down so you could be free.

Tears rolling and I accepted Him into my heart,
He wipes my face and says, "Now let me do my part".

Broken and despair no more I was,
I fought, prayed, shouted, even cried for the cause,
He loved me just as I was.

Many times, I rejected that caring soul to follow my own way,
But no more dismissal I have given him my life today.

Broken and despair he found me,
He chased, pursued and now I can live in victory.

BUT I MUST ASK– 6/13/21.

THEY CAME AND GATHERED, AND A FRAGRANCE WAS IN
THE AIR,
BUT I MUST ASK, IS MY PRESENCE THERE?

I WAS CHECKING THE SOUND THAT WAS IN THE ROOM,
BUT I MUST ASK, DO I NEED TO COME DO A SWEEP
THROUGH?

I WAS WATCHING WHAT WAS BEING PRESENTED TO ME,
BUT I MUST ASK, DO MY PEOPLE REALLY HAVE THE
VICTORY?

I WAS THERE SITTING IN THE ROOM TO SEE IF THEY REALLY
LOVED ME,
BUT I MUST ASK, DO THEY REALLY GIVE ME TRUE
INTIMACY?

THEY HAVE LEANED ON WHAT THEY SAID THAT THEY AT
LEAST KNOW,
BUT I MUST ASK, DO THEY KNOW ME, OR DO THEY ONLY
CARE ABOUT THEIR NEW HAIRDO.

THEY GATHERED AND SHOWED THEMSELVES TO BE
FRIENDLY TO EACH OTHER,
BUT I MUST ASK, WHY DID YOU LEAVE THAT SISTER AND
TALK ABOUT YOUR BROTHER.

HOW CAN YOU SAY YOU LOVE ME WHOM YOU HAVE NOT
SEEN AND HATE ONE ANOTHER EVERY DAY,

Psalms Of A Prophet

Subtitle: In The Midst of It All I got an Answer

BUT I MUST ASK, DO YOU CARRY ME, OR DO YOU GO
YOUR OWN WAY?

THEY CALL ME LORD AND SAY I REIGN IN YOUR LIFE,
BUT I MUST ASK, WHEN WAS THE LAST TIME YOU MADE A
SACRIFICE?

IT SOUNDS GOOD WHEN YOU FINAGLE YOUR WORDS WITH
SWEET HONEY,
BUT I MUST ASK WHEN I ASK YOU TO PRAY WHY DID YOU
ACT FUNNY?

IN FRONT OF MY PEOPLE, YOU MAKE IT'S AS IF YOU HAVE
ARRIVED WITH SO MUCH POWER,
BUT I MUST ASK WHY ARE YOU HOLDING ON TO THE
HURT AS YOUR STRONG TOWER?

I AM CALLING YOU TO SUBMIT YOUR WILLS TO ME,
AND I WILL SHOW YOU A LIFE OF VICTORY,
BUT I MUST ASK DO YOU REALLY LOVE ME?

Created Just 4 Me

This place where I am if unfamiliar to me,
I see animals, angels, trees, and water roaming around free.

It was peace there one great big harmony,
Could this be the place that God created just for me?

Psalms Of A Prophet

Subtitle: In The Midst of It All I got an Answer

I never knew that man, angels, and animals could get along one
with another,
Where is this place that I am in it's like no other.

As I looked around, I saw a world free from chaos,
Not pimps and players trying to earn a buck by rolling dice.

Low I heard a voice that spoke to me that said, "Son I created
something just for you".
Me I am not worthy to receive anything after all that I have done to
you.

When you came to me, I forgave you never to remember it no
more,
God, you forgave me every little sin right down to the core.

Tears filled my eyes that a God could love me that much to blotted
out my mess,
For him to look at me and say, from your mother's womb I have
called you blessed.

He led me in this room where it was peaceful there,
He told me to lay down; I want to share with you on how much I
care.

I laid down on this bed of clouds that was created just for me,
As God talked to me and shared his heart, somehow, I went right to
sleep.

Psalms Of A Prophet

Subtitle: In The Midst of It All I got an Answer

As I slept, I could feel the warm embrace of my loving father that has given me rest,
I heard him sing to me and I created in you words of wisdom and I called you blessed.

As I woke up from the presence of God to my surprise, he said, "I have created something just for you,"
I was curious because I was undeserving of anything that God wanted to do.

I looked to my right there was another person in the room,
God told this person daughter I have created your groom.

Father, what have I done this time?
I knew you were in need of a blessing, so I gave you a one of a kind.

God took my hand and hers and place it in mine,
Look at me and said that it was ordained all of the time.

She smiled and said man of God I'll follow wherever God would lead you,
He told me how much you sacrifice to do what he has called you to do.

He told me carry you and to trust you to lead,
For I have always been strong, never allowing anyone to get close to me.

But one day God spoke to me and said, "I created you as a bride so love on me."

Psalms Of A Prophet

Subtitle: In The Midst of It All I got an Answer

I had to give me up and be intimate with the one that set me free.

Now that I am here, I realize why I could not love any but God
because he created you just for me,
I cried the whole time that God has considered me.

This beautiful princess that was blessed with favor,
God said for the harvest is great but there is little that labor.

I chose the both of you for such a time as this,
To lead my sheep into my kingdom so they would be on the
heavenly VIP list.

My bride and I was overwhelmed that God have found us,
That the angels in heaven shouted out from morning until dusk.

Thank you, God, for loving me,
That you created Eve just for me.

Death has come!

Psalms Of A Prophet

Subtitle: In The Midst of It All I got an Answer

When death surrounds you, can you feel it taunting you?
Or do you turn your back like it doesn't faze you?

You feel as though you can escape anything that comes your way,
But do you realize today can be your last day?

You go forth destroying happy homes like it is alright,
But guess what I death come for you tonight!

You go around hurting the innocence of a child,
But I death, see you acting wild!

You stand by ready to pounce on your prey,
But I death is putting a stop to that; I'm serving your death on a tray.

You call on me when you want to harm others,
But tonight, I death is sticking to you like your brother.

There will be no escape from the tormenting hell that you are going to be
face with today,
I death says," that this payback in every way"!

You made your bed, so now you have lie in its misery,
While others are called up to see God over in glory.

Hell is not a pretty place for no one to be,
But so many are playing around you see,
Death has come and knocked at your door and there is no escape for you
and me.

Psalms Of A Prophet

Subtitle: In The Midst of It All I got an Answer

DISTURBED!

I LOOKED UP TO HEAVEN AND A FROWN ON GOD'S FACE,

I SAID, "WHATS THE MATTER DADDY?"

HE SAID, "I HAVE TOO MUCH GRACE".

I GOT VERY WORRIED, FOR I KNEW HE WAS MAD,

FOR I KNEW THAT HIM AND Satan WAS ON A WAR PATH!

I TOLD GOD, "HEAR AM I SEND ME",

HE SAID, "NO, FOR I'M ON MY WAY BACK YOU SEE".

I'VE HAD ENOUGH WITH SIN AND PAIN,

I SENT MY SON THE FIRST TIME, THAT SALVATION THEY MUST GAIN.

Psalms Of A Prophet

Subtitle: In The Midst of It All I got an Answer

MY SPIRIT GOT VERY DISTURBED,

FOR I KNEW WHEN GOD SAID, "HE HAD ENOUGH",

FOR HE WOULD SEND FIRE FROM HEAVEN ON THE SMOOTHED PLAINS AND ROUGH,

GOD IS COMING FOR HIS BRIDES,

WILL YOU BE READY OR WILL KEEP THAT PRIDE?

Do you, or Does It?

Do you hear what I hear?
A world in chaos is in the ear.

Can you see what I see?
A child in bended knees begging to be free.

What happened to us? Where did we go wrong?
Father forgive us; we have been away for far too long.

I can't even imagine how you can make something out of dirt to be.
To create something beautiful within a messed-up person like me.

Do you hear what I hear?
Somebody's mother has been beaten and is living in fear.

Psalms Of A Prophet

Subtitle: In The Midst of It All I got an Answer

Do we care what happens to the little ones?
Evidently, we don't. Is that that why we walk with guns?

I could remember when we would lay our lives down for you.
Now we are waiting for the next time I can use you.

Can you understand the pain that I am carrying in me?
Does it bother you when I turn to the left or the right there is my enemy?

Does it bother you that your sister's having abortions?
Or do you enjoy being caught in the commotion?

Does it bother you that your brother is strung out on drugs?
Or that your children have never felt a real hug?

Does it bother you that your sister turns to a man that hits her every night?
Or if your brother will ever walk in the light?

My heart aches to know I could have helped but would not.
Is that why I am beaten, battered, and bruised and it won't stop?

Why did we turn away from that which we know?
When God said, "Come to me and I'll wash you whiter than snow.

God, I'm sorry for walking without you,
Can you ever forgive me and show me what to do?

I knew eventually you would turn back to me,
In the midst of it all, I have an answer for thee,
Is there anything too hard for me?

From Darkness to Light

A puff of clouds hangs over my head trying to figure out why I am down,
Not wearing the smile, I once had but wearing a frown.

Psalms Of A Prophet

Subtitle: In The Midst of It All I got an Answer

Tears will not come, and I don't understand why,
What have I done to be on standby?

I cannot hear the answers anymore from the spirit I once knew,
Now just silence and the stillness with no drive to make it on through.

A knock at the door, "hello who's there"?
A tap on my shoulders saying, "It is I the Almighty that cares'.

I cannot face him for what he might say,
But I know he told me that He would guide me along the way.

Still, I just cannot face Him,
For I knew that my light had gone dim.

He said son, why live in fear of your life?
Tears flowed because I realized I hadn't made a sacrifice.

Where did I go wrong, why did I leave him?
Today my son give it up and step out on that limb.

The tunnel of darkness I was in, I could barely see the light,
Arise my child and hold on, then fight, fight, fight!

Felt like I just could not do it, I did not want to fall,
How else will you learn if you never hit a few walls?

Gradually I was gaining my confidence back,
Jesus said, "I will hold you, so you want fall off track".

I made it! I can see the lights,
Today I declare I shall rise above all the darkest nights.

I must fight in order to see the one, who died for me,
To see the end was joy for me you see.

Psalms Of A Prophet

Subtitle: In The Midst of It All I got an Answer

I'm glad he took the time to see about me,
Now I can live in freedom and take the time to walk in liberty.

From darkness to light was a step for me,
To accept myself as the man of God and walk in integrity, that is what Jesus did for me.

God Is Concerned About You-

When I called you, you did not answer me,
When I called you by name you ignored me,
And now you are crying to be set free.

I heard you in your sincerity,
I just wanted to challenge your integrity.

I've called you my chosen vessel to be used,
To go get my people so they can be rescued.

But when I told you go, you found an excuse,
Now you have sunk into the deep and now you need to be rescued.

Keep my commandments and live,
You said that it's better to receive than to give.

You have twisted my word for your own personal gain,
Now my child you will know that there is power in my name.

Once I put your name on the scroll of life,
Now you are sold into slavery for such a high price.

Psalms Of A Prophet

Subtitle: In The Midst of It All I got an Answer

You and I don't communicate any more,
You are like a fish in a lake attracted to the lure.

You spoke yourself into a situation that has become part of you,
So how can you say that you love me when you don't know what to do?

When you don't follow me, you are under the law,
The enemy has set you up and hit you right in the jaw.

How long will you play this game?
In and out thinking you are going to have great fame.

This relationship has caused you to be a stranger to me,
So now we must get reacquainted so you will know who I am to thee.

For you were brought with a mighty big price,
I gave my only son to die for you for a big sacrifice, YOUR LIFE!

Where did you and I go wrong?
You tipped out on me to be with another lover of the world, and I must
now tell you so long.

It hurts me to see you go your way,
Sin I cannot look on, my child have a nice day.

You can't think you will get my inheritance and you have another father in
your life,
You expected for me to turn my head and allow you to look at my back to
stab me with a knife.

I am omnipresence; I see everything that you do,
Oh, disobedient child, what do you think I expect from you?

Psalms Of A Prophet

Subtitle: In The Midst of It All I got an Answer

Until you turn from the things that displeases me,
We are no more connected until you truly repent and be set free,
Until then I don't know thee.

GOD, YOU GET ON MY NERVES- PART 1

God, you get on my nerves even though you knew that I would love you,
Even when I turned away you still pulled me through.

You take me through all these crazy changes that I didn't not understand,
but you knew that I wouldn't let go of your hand.

God, you get on my nerves even when you put objects in my pathway,
the rejection I experienced from day to day,
You knew already that all I would do is pray.

Where were you when your child had pills in his hands to take his life,
I know I heard you speak and said my son I have already paid the price.

but wait God where were you while I was being raped,
But I saw angels and your voice said I have made a way for you to escape.

God, you get on my nerves why wouldn't you let me fit in with others I knew,
You said to me you were chosen from your mother's womb, so you don't get to do what you do.

Psalms Of A Prophet

Subtitle: In The Midst of It All I got an Answer

OK where were you when my father was killed in that car crash,
even while I was taking care of others I still was treated like trash.

Oh, remember while I was in your church serving you,
the pastor said," you will never be free from the sin that you do",
still, you spoke to me and said, "hey son I love you"!

God, you get on my nerves that you could love someone like me,
my dear child my grace is sufficient for thee you see.

OK what about I was just being kind and you let that person put that
gun to my head,
I was there with you and by my spirit you were led.

You allow me to be broken just looking for someone to love me and
behold another one pinned me down, pull my clothes off and split
me,
and I heard you say I will never leave you nor for sake thee.

God, you get on my nerves that you knew that I would still love you,
my love, you are the essence of my unfailing residue.

Regardless of the pain that you have felt over and over again,
that I would die for you and wipe out all of your sin.

Thank you, God, for getting on my nerves every step of the way,
for you knew that my steps were ordered every moment and every
day.

Keep getting on my nerves Lord, my life was set up to please you,
even the pain, rejection, rape, abuse, the loss of my father, brought
me through,

Psalms Of A Prophet

Subtitle: In The Midst of It All I got an Answer

just so I know that I belong to you.

Written by: Dr. Derrick R Zachary
Time: 1142pm
Date: 06/15/2022

GOD, YOU GET ON MY NERVES:

PART 2

Psalms Of A Prophet

Subtitle: In The Midst of It All I got an Answer

OK God it's me again I have a few concerns with these crazy folks,
Why must I be kind and sweet when they continue to poke.

God, you get on my nerves where were you when this person had the
audacity to put their hands in my face,
My child did I not say I will repay, but in my time and in my place.

OK I got you but what about when this stupid person decided to slap
me,
Have I ever left you? Did I not protect you from the tragedy?

God, you get on my nerves how many times you expect me to
forgive these so-called Saints that use your name,
Forgive over and over again, it's not for them but for you not to go
insane.

OK you doing too much God, can I just be like your boy Saul?
Oh, you forgot he had an experience with me, and I changed his
name to Paul.

God, you get on my nerves every time I want to do right evilness
always present with me,
That's because you won't let your flesh die, you too busy walking to
your own trickery.

But God wait, I have loved my enemies many times after time and
yet they use my identity to get ahead,
Yes, I know, you keep opening the door to something that was
already dead.

God, you get on my nerves I reached out for help but all I got was I
can't help you,

Psalms Of A Prophet

Subtitle: In The Midst of It All I got an Answer

But did you come to me if you would have you would have made it through.

God, you get on my nerves somehow you knew I would still find my way to you,
Again, my child, I knew who you were before you knew what to do.

After all I've been through you still keep your hands on little old me,
I knew that you would be the greatest leader that would represent victory.

You have overcome the hardship even when you thought that you couldn't do it,
But I have given you the ability to take hit after hit, so you will pull through it.

I know I have worked your last nerves since the day you were born on this earth,
But I say to you, I spoke favor on you since the day of your birth.

Thank you, God, for getting on my nerves every day,
It caused me to seek you out in a very special way.

Never shall I forget the love you gave to me,
It was because of your son Jesus that I can live in victory,
Now my son save my people and stop worrying me!

Written By: Dr Derrick Zachary
Date: July 7,2022
Time:2:30pm

Psalms Of A Prophet

Subtitle: In The Midst of It All I got an Answer

HE TOUCH ME

Softly he touches the depth of me.
Can it be real? Someone that makes me be.

He touches the very inner me.
He looks at me and sees a great destiny.

When I'm burnt out, he allows me to rest.
He allows me to vent so I can be my best.

You ever wonder why he cares so much.

Psalms Of A Prophet

Subtitle: In The Midst of It All I got an Answer

He makes sure that there isn't one soul he hasn't touched.

When my body hurts, he removes the pain.
He says, "Hey son, hey daughter you are not going insane."

Even when I'm caught in life's affairs.
He lets me know to cast all my cares on him for he cares.

He makes me laugh at the very thought of him.
He and I have gotten very close even when my life is on a limb.

He knows how fragile I am.
He never leaves me. He keeps me in the palm of his hand.

There are days when I just want to be a baby.
He allows me to be that for a day and calls him daddy.

There are days when the nights seem so dark.
But he steps in and it's like heaven in an open park.

He is the only one I know that can be in more than one place.
He is like superman except with a smile on his face.

When he touches me, my body quivers with excitement.
It's like he stares at your soul making a statement.

He was drawn to me, it's like he knew everything about me.
I was drawn to him because it fit my destiny.

He's quite mysterious; only giving bits and pieces of who he is.
He rocks everyone's world. That's just who he is.

He is the sweetest I know.

Psalms Of A Prophet

Subtitle: In The Midst of It All I got an Answer

He can make it rain in one area and in the other area snow.

It's just something about the way He touches me.
Whatever is bothering me he reminds me that is not your destiny. He and I were just meant to be.

Does he have an agenda for my life?
Naw, He reminded me that he already paid the ultimate price.

I love him because he is the only one that knows the depth of me.
The inside and out all praise to Thee.

What made me fall in love with him was the way he touched me.
And for that Him and I will always be soul mates.
That was our destiny.

HEAR ME OH ZION- 12/9/12

Hear me oh Zion I am calling you,
hear me little children I will see you through.

Hear me Oh Zion they came to judge you,
They are judging to see what character is in you.

Hear me oh Zion I am refining you with gold,
Know you will no longer be on display are to be sold.

I will not cut you off from me,
but oh, Zion it's time you rise and walk in victory!

Hear me oh Zion my people have turned to sin,
don't you realize that without me you cannot win.

I am calling you back to me in this season,

Psalms Of A Prophet

Subtitle: In The Midst of It All I got an Answer

If you fail to listen to my voice, you will be brought up on charges for all of the right reasons.

I have given you a clear vision of who I am,
Why are you busy trying to please Uncle Sam?

I sealed you in my blood so death can pass you by,
and yet with presented with the question are you a Christian that stood by and denied?

I sought you out and hand-picked you from the womb,
Yet Zion you are walking around like a body locked up in a tomb.

I presented Jesus for you so you can have new life,
Was it all in vain that he continues to make the sacrifice?

Behold I will not refine you with silver nor gold,
behold I will refine you with the garment of praise so that you will be made whole.

Hear me O Zion I am chasing after you,
I am tired of running behind someone that chooses to be sad and blue.

Psalms Of A Prophet

Subtitle: In The Midst of It All I got an Answer

I am establishing you with Kingdom authority to keep your
focus on track,
But now I'm snatching the keys and all that I gave you
back.

Hear me O Zion I am calling you to a place that I will give
to you,
For I chose you from the beginning to worship me, that is
what you do.

No longer will you be caught up in the cares of this world,
I call my remnant, my hidden jewels the one I call my Pearl.

Hear me O Zion I am coming soon,
no man knows the hour that I will return but it might just
be at noon.

Hear me oh Zion let that mess down,
stop being tricked by the foolishness around town.

Rise, stand conquer and defeat,
gird your loins, tie your shoes today I have given you a new
beat.

Psalms Of A Prophet

Subtitle: In The Midst of It All I got an Answer

Hear Ye the Sound

2/21/15.

Here you the sound in the earth,
for I called you by name from the dirt.

Hear you the sound in the air,
for I the Lord came to repair.

Hear you the sound in the wind,
for I made you whole so come out of sin.

Loveth thou me? please feed my lambs,
for this is not a game where the Saints against the Rams.

There is a war going forward do you not see?
Why have you not come unto me.

Psalms Of A Prophet

Subtitle: In The Midst of It All I got an Answer

I am your Redeemer the one that live it in you,
I am the lion of Judah that knows exactly what to do.

I grew through the adversities to be a chosen 1,
I never tried to destroy you by using a gun.

My cry was loud, and the pain was intense,
but my suffering carried me with no pretense.

They try to erase your identity beyond repair,
but what I created on the wheel was the heart of care.

Hear the sound the blood has been shed,
There are rumors of war and many warriors have bled.

I am the supplier of all your needs,
Did you not know that the ground produces seeds?

I am the word that health thee,
Give up the excuses and run unto me.

Flip flop people I cannot use,
but I charge you to handle the abuse.

You have been distracted by cares of this world,
how long will you be stuck in this swirl.

Your life is like a pig pen just waddling in your mess,
come out of bondage for I called you to be blessed.

You've been hanging with fakeness and the witches,

Psalms Of A Prophet

Subtitle: In The Midst of It All I got an Answer

but be careful of their life is full of ditches.

From the belly I form you for a greater work,
but you live life trying to twist and to twerk.

for I am coming like a thief in the night,
but you will be caught in darkness rather than light.

My leaders I put to declare my word have left the scene,
but my remnant is rising preaching repentance and be clean.

Heart of my heart, for it cries for you,
stop confusing me with Buddha for I am the truth.

My ears are open to you if you call,
I am not far away I am your all and all.

Cry aloud and spare not for I am raging war,
my anointing was never to be kept in a jar.

My thoughts of you are good and not of bad,
hold your head up and stop looking so sad.

Psalms Of A Prophet

Subtitle: In The Midst of It All I got an Answer

I am A Better Me
8/30/2010

A troubled mine brought me here,

When I came, I had a lot of tears.

I didn't want to be here at all,

I would rather spend time playing football.

I could see the tears in my father's eyes,

I was so sad when he said goodbye.

Every week I am excited to see them come,

for I know in me the battle is already won. I am much better now I think,

my attitude has improved, it doesn't stink.

I'm better because everyone believed in me,

Psalms Of A Prophet

Subtitle: In The Midst of It All I got an Answer

Because of that I can control my destiny.

I am almost out of this place,

I will make an impact on the world,

look the bad right in the face.

I am proud to have parents that care,

Not all I have to do is my part and my share.

Written by: Derrick Zachary and William Zachary-Downs (Son)

I am Waiting.6/5/11

I am asking the house to invite me in, but they would not let me in there,

I stood at the door knocking asking how much more do I have to bear?

I stood by as I watched the elite pass right by,

had their heads lift it up nose in the air like they have arrived!

Psalms Of A Prophet

Subtitle: In The Midst of It All I got an Answer

They could not feel my spirit because they had no presence of
the Holy Ghost within them,
Their light used to shine but it's just grown dim and dim.

They no longer hear my voice called out their name,
They're just interested in the money and right now the Fame!

I have a hurting people waiting to be fed the word,
but they have prepared their own documentations clarity it's not
my voice they heard.

Wow I'm amazed that they stop communicating with me,
yet they are declaring and decreeing that they love me!

The drunks, the homeless, the prostitutes, they walked right by
would not lend a helping hand,
must I send another warning and destroy this sinful land?

God my father I died once I am not doing it again to save a
rebellious people that don't want you,
you are about to sound the alarm they won't be ready oh God
what to do?

Is it worth saving these dogs that will not change?
Oh God I am sorry does this seem strange?

Who or what has poisoned the souls?
The same old serpent that left them out in the cold!

Psalms Of A Prophet

Subtitle: In The Midst of It All I got an Answer

I have warned them to watch and pray,
instead, they said in their heart I am going to do it my own
way.

Oh, I see a crack I might be able to get in,
No, that lying pastor said it was OK to do that sin!

Wait what is it that I hear someone in the corner that actually
loves me,
I got to use that one to be a light that one will not lose their
identity.

Look how they love us father, can I bless them in an unusual
way?
Go ahead son rain down favor on them today,
let the world know that I'm still the able I am the Potter, and
they are the clay.

I have remnants set aside for just this reason,
There is one in every place that you will go, it will be their
season.

Choose today which side you choose to be on,
stay there and fight for you and I have the true DNA bond.

Psalms Of A Prophet

Subtitle: In The Midst of It All I got an Answer

 I AM

I am a smooth God that can make the rough made without a scratch,

I am the Rose of Sharon in the midst of a sticky thorn patch.

I am the coverer over all your mess,

I am the one that stands back and says I called them blessed.

I am the mender of everything broken into pieces,

Psalms Of A Prophet

Subtitle: In The Midst of It All I got an Answer

I am the God that has called every species.

I am the true vine that produces good seed,

I am also the God that will separate the wheat from the weed.

I am the God that will cause you to push past your pain,

I am also the same God that will keep you from going insane.

I am a jealous God that will have no other before me,

I am the God that hates sin but called integrity.

I am a walking miracle walking with action,

I am a God that will add and do subtraction.

I called you even before you knew me,

I place worship in you not the pleasure of iniquity.

I am the Lord, i love to bless my sheep,

I am the God that is always up I never sleep.

Give ear to my words I want to bless you,

stop consulting with astrologers trying to find out what to do.

I am the God who listens closely to your tears that you cry,

but I speak to you, you shall live and not die.

There be many that say who will show us any good this day,

fool if you were in prayer, you know I always make a way.

Psalms Of A Prophet

Subtitle: In The Midst of It All I got an Answer

I am the Great I Am that is my name,

Are seeking me or do you just want the fame?

I know your way that you go with even when you think I do not know,

for I the Lord your God spoke it and it was so.

I am a smooth God that's what I do,

So today, am I the God for you?

Written: 6/9/2011

Psalms Of A Prophet
Subtitle: In The Midst of It All I got an Answer

I GOT YOU COVERED- 7/28/12

I cover you with my wings,
while the angels in heaven begin to sing.

While you were going through, I put you in my hands,
while everyone else around you were as sinking sand.

I call you for purpose and destiny,
It's not a choice in the matter I've given you victory.

Stand up and square your shoulders it's time to fight,
for I am swift and know how to maneuver through the night.

I thought of you while you were in your mother's womb,
I covered you when they tried to put you in the tomb.

I got you covered if you allow me to,
Stop relying on your flesh and I'll let me do it for you.

I have need of thee in this season,

Psalms Of A Prophet

Subtitle: In The Midst of It All I got an Answer

There will be many that will cause treason.

But I shall hide thee under my wing,
I will reveal it to you when you realize I got everything.

here I am God standing in need of thee.
Can you hear what I hear, can you hear me?

My child I hear you I put my glory cloud to cover you,
Bring your worship and Thanksgiving, that's all you must do.

No longer will you be in the storm that's been attacking you,
you will soar above elements that what I am going to do.

Straighten up I'm putting food back in your Hubbard,
hey, guess what I've got you covered!

I HAVE A TESTIMONY

I have a testimony so let me tell it,
You can't tell it for me so let me do it.

I have spent time in this place you are in,
It became a friend of mine that fight within,
Telling me you know you will never win.

It had me trapped on the inside,
That thing called suicide stayed glued to my side.

Time and time again suicide tried to take my life,
But my other friend name Jesus, said no my child I have already paid the price.

Psalms Of A Prophet

Subtitle: In The Midst of It All I got an Answer

The feeling that came over me was a spirit of relief,
Now that I am walking in liberty, I have ridiculous belief.

I have a testimony can I take sometimes out and tell you,
To tell you how many times the lord has come to my rescue.

Remember those times when you had those crazy nightmares,
Oh, had those days too of life truth or dares.

When being attack in your sleep from different spirits sent from hell,
All the fighting you were doing as you're falling you gave out a great big yell.

When your life is all most shattered in your dream,
And you woke up in a major sweat like water flowing in a stream.

Been there and did that it's the attack of enemy to help you fall off track,
But God said no my child I got your back.

Seems like you get deliver from one thing and then get trapped in other,
Then you find yourself dealing with too many lovers.

Your mind says, "What I don't understand",
Let me continue to testify, so your mind can be untwined from rope strands.

Have you ever felt like hurting someone to the point of death?
That you got with different kinds of people and played life little bets.

You wonder why this has happen to you,
Why would they rape me and beat me until I am black and blue?
Been there, let me continue to testify unto you.

Psalms Of A Prophet

Subtitle: In The Midst of It All I got an Answer

Maybe there was something on me that attracted them to me,
It was the innocence of my spirit to break the depth of me.

I didn't understand how I could put myself in harm's way,
Nothing that I did wrong to have someone take away my bright day.

There scent I can still smell on me,
My thoughts are to destroy, annulate every dead thing that comes in
contact with me.

All I heard was it was your fault that this happen to you,
But I could not understand if you have not experience how can you
understand what I am going through.

What I did I do so wrong to go through something like that,
Because the enemy peeked inside your future and knew that you were
going to give the devil his tools back.

So, he did the unthinkable and tried to rape you of your identity,
But Jesus said I die so you may have life more abundantly.

You just can't begin to conceive it your mind,
How can one person go through so much in just a short time?
Ooh can I please testify!!

I have a testimony that is out of this world,
Have been to hell and back even had to chuck a couple of hurls.

But somehow, I managed to come out on top,
Despite suicide, nightmares, and rape as long as I got Jesus I can't be stop.

Many said that I was not going to be nobody,

Psalms Of A Prophet

Subtitle: In The Midst of It All I got an Answer

But somehow, I overcame what they said and became somebody.

The secret was having a conversation with Christ about what I was going through,
You know what he did, he touched my mouth, so praise is what is do.

How can one person praise god like that,
Does it matter how I got there, I have yet to lose track.

Can I take a minute to tell you, my testimony?
I have lived life for everyone else until I became phony.

Now why would I say something like that knowing what god has done for me?
Because it was the very ones that said they loved me, but really what they wanted was intimacy.

You see dealing with life's little crooks and turns,
The people I trusted and gave my heart to just lied to me and I got burned.

The more I said I wasn't going to participate between sheets,
I seem to find myself in the midst of the heat.

I'll say I am not going to fornicate anymore,
But I yield to temptation because I just wanted to feel nice and get a little more.

You see I've been where you at,
It takes prayer, fasting, and getting my life intact.

Please let me tell my testimony of what I've been through,
I planned to escape from everything the world, my family, and even you.

Psalms Of A Prophet

Subtitle: In The Midst of It All I got an Answer

Why? Because I was tired of falling back in the same situation over and over again,
I didn't know why, but the Lord revealed to me that it was because of sin.

You see not all the time you are aware that there is sin,
You see when you play with Christ you put your life on a limb.

My testimony does not just stop there,
I have even had sex with those professing that Christ cares.

They care enough just to get me in the bed,
I was so angry at myself that all I could see was red.

How long will this cycle last?
When I learn to live for the future and stop going into the past.

Can I move from the past? Can I let it go?
It's either heaven or hell or the lake of fire with a forever flow.

Did I want to make the choice to live or to die?
So many times, I did, I chose to survive.

Oh, it didn't stop there; it was so easy to do wrong,
But the more I did it, the more my blessing was prolonged.

I could not figure out why I kept falling,
I always found myself in a corner balling.

It hurt my spirit and my mind to end up here,
But realize the more I wanted to do right evil was present right there.

I fought and fought to try to make it through the day,

Psalms Of A Prophet

Subtitle: In The Midst of It All I got an Answer

But the spirit of depression came on me and I backed a away.

But the lord spoke to me saying, "Why are you backing up when you know you can stand,
I knew in myself I could, the Lord said, "here child a helping hand."

The hand of mercy was stretched out to me,
Stand still and see the salvation of the Lord and begin to walk in your destiny.

My destiny leads me here to tell my testimony to you,
I overcame by the blood of the lamb and by the words I testified to you,
You can make it my brothers and sister all the way through,
Be free in Christ that's what the lord expects from you,
I have a testimony and I hope that it has been delivered to you.

Psalms Of A Prophet

Subtitle: In The Midst of It All I got an Answer

I Long for YOU -6/8/13

A soldier needs to be afraid of the fight,
pick yourself up I want to spend some time with you
tonight.

I brought you out of the ashes of dead things,
You are my son, but you have turned to the former things.

How can we be father and son when you spend no time
with me,
I want to be there for you, but you have turned your back
on daddy.

I remember you used to look up to me as your superhero,
Now you treat me as though I am a zero.

I cry for you every day because I know who you are,
but you took on another identity and now you are behind
bars.

You come to me only when you need me to do you a
favor,
but my harvest is great but there is none that labors.

I seek for you and cannot find you,
Why have you hidden yourself when you know what to
do?

Who told you, you were naked when it wasn't a problem
before,

Psalms Of A Prophet

Subtitle: In The Midst of It All I got an Answer

now you are ashamed defeated broken living your life in gore.

I bid you to come home I long to be with thee,
I heard your cry come spend time with me.

What is the stronghold that has you so bound,
Stop using excuses just because you want to play around.

Add my table there is plenty to eat,
Why do you choose garbage then eat this good meat?

Come back to your first love,
I ascended upon you as this beautiful white dove.

The honey is so sweet as I see who you can be,
My heart is heavy with the weight that I carry for you to be with me.

If I Decided

If I decided to dry up all your funds,
will you stop serving me and start picking up guns?

Psalms Of A Prophet

Subtitle: In The Midst of It All I got an Answer

If I decided to stop blessing you for just a moment, what would you do?
Would you curse me and leave the one that I love you?

If I decided to put you on the streets, can you still trust me?
Or would you stop being faithful and walk around to your own beat?

If I decided to strike your body with sickness, would you still preach?
Or would you fold up the word and say, "God lies that's what I am going to teach?"

If I decided to tell you what I really need from you could you accept what I say?
or would you fall asleep on me day by day?

If I decided to snatch the job you are holding on to, would I still be Lord over your life?
Would you stand on the corner presenting your body as a sacrifice?

Psalms Of A Prophet

Subtitle: In The Midst of It All I got an Answer

If I decided not to bless anyone anymore, would you still worship me?
Hey Lord, despite it all I will still bless thee,
because I died to me, I chose to pick up my cross to follow thee,
I decided Lord to be all that you have called me to be,
Victorious, prosperous, and mighty in integrity.

If I told you

Praise is what I long for,
Why have my people put me to the side?
Yet it is I who them to survive.

If I told you to give it all up, could you?
Or would you find an excuse for what you can't do?

Why want you worship me?
And yet you chose Egypt instead of being free.

You have lost your way,
When I was a pillar of fire by night and a cloud of smoke by day.

I want you to have life more abundantly, in every way,
I had so much for you, I don't think you deserve it today.

Psalms Of A Prophet

Subtitle: In The Midst of It All I got an Answer

If I told you to give your brother a helping hand, could you?
I don't think you can because you are selfish, twisted, and don't have a clue.

I created you in one day and it repented me that I ever did,
What went wrong; you gambled on your life and now you are up for bid.

You didn't think I knew every time you cheated on me?
You must be crazy for I am God Almighty!

What happened to our relationship? Why is it that we don't talk?
Can we have time; can we go for a walk?

Wait a minute, since when do I compromise who I am to get to know you,
I am the first and the last how about I'm sick of you!

You love me today hate me tomorrow what kind of a relationship is that?
Maybe you thought you had nine lives you know like a cat.

This relationship is ending; I am tired of chasing you to be with me,
Now you are free to live your life with the enemy.

So now that I am not there for you,
Process this, you and I are through,
I found someone that is into me,
Okay bye-bye there is no more you.

In the wilderness I hear your voice

Wondering around in the wilderness for years and years,
Searching to find an answer to remove my darkest fears.

Surrounded by the guilt and anguish of my past,
Carrying the hurt of pain, please tell me how long can this last?

Psalms Of A Prophet

Subtitle: In The Midst of It All I got an Answer

Battered and scorn by the memories in my mind,
I heard nothing, just standing still like the end of time.

My heart so heavy and I cried out of despair,
Saying Lord, "hello is anyone there?"

Deep down I knew I was tired of the guilt inside,
Still, no one answered me, just the tricks that were playing on my mind.

In this empty place I've began to be broken in two,
Then I heard just a still small voice said, "I Love you."

Years of tricks and deceit was playing on my emotions,
Until I heard in the wind, can we have some devotion?

Could it be someone answer my call,
I see you my child did you fall?

I cried to him; I cannot take it anymore!
I'm sick of the disappointments and life's little gores.

I sought you for guidance and all I got was the door shut,
I knew something would happen to me I felt it in my gut.

Why did you take me down this road of pain?
Why do I feel at times I'm about to go insane.

Did I do something wrong that would have caused me to go through this?
Did you search your scroll and remove my name from the list?

Let me say to child I never left you,
I was with you even when you were going through.

Psalms Of A Prophet

Subtitle: In The Midst of It All I got an Answer

The test I put you through was for you to know why I paid the price,
You must surrender and make the ultimate sacrifice.

Pick up your cross and deny you,
How can I show you what to do if you are not willing to die to you?

When I went to Calvary it was because of you,
You went to the cross, but you did not give up you.

You say you want to do my will with all your heart,
It's your heart that has not been changed that is the start.

You can wonder years in this wilderness and never get out,
It's your fears that keep you in bondage, come on want you give me a shout.

Cast all your cares on me,
Then I'll take from the wilderness to the land that I promise thee.

I fasted for forty days and forty nights to hear a word for me,
But you know what I hear, deliver the people so they can be free.

I know this place this place does not feel good to you,
But ask yourself this, "would I rather be a bondage breaker or someone that can't do?"

So, this wilderness you are in, hear my voice,
I chose you from your mother womb, so your destiny is set, it's not a choice.

Seek my face and turn from your wicked ways,
And I will add life to you and prolong your days.

Psalms Of A Prophet

Subtitle: In The Midst of It All I got an Answer

Hear my voice this day, I called you Holy and free,
All fear is removed this day now go in peace.

INTRODUCTION OF
BEING MISSED

Apostle Pamela Terry

Psalms Of A Prophet

Subtitle: In The Midst of It All I got an Answer

Written by: Apostle Dr. Derrick R Zachary

(Michael)

5/4/2021

Time: 8:35pm

Psalms Of A Prophet

Subtitle: In The Midst of It All I got an Answer

We were introduced over a phone call,
Right at that moment the enemy wanted you to fall.

Instantly the Lord spoke to me to give a word to you,
That you would be unstoppable and that you will make it
through.

You were in a place as if your back was against the wall,
But the father clearly spoke, Pamela, it is you that walk with
this call.

He gave you a smile that could light up a room,
The undeniable word that was over your life was preparing
you for the groom.

The day we met you said I reminded you of your little brother
Michael he you had loss,
that God gave you a replacement you just knew you were the
boss.

Out of your struggles birth out Southern Outreach,
that the oil of the pen was how you would teach.

Psalms Of A Prophet

Subtitle: In The Midst of It All I got an Answer

The very first conference you had was one to put on the books,
we were busting Devils up and down that we got in every little crooks.

It was in that year the Lord spoke 21 days breakthrough would happen just do not faint,
the Holy Ghost would prove himself and a revival of healing would come to the Saints.

Our bond was just like as strong as gorilla glue,
As people saw the oil on you, they still did not have a clue.

Then you got up the nerves to get up and moved on a brother,
met a man that you called **Exquisite** because he was like no other.

I had to give my stamp of approval on him if he was going to be with you,
he called you **Pretty Eyes** and you shine like you just got a new hairdo.

Psalms Of A Prophet

Subtitle: In The Midst of It All I got an Answer

Then comes the wedding day I watched all the people make a
fuss,
but it went off without a glitch, so I danced to the song "*Lord
rain on us*".

Now your journey has taken us again to another place,
Now you are standing with your ultimate lover of all things
face to face.

Take your rest you deserve it **Ms. Pretty Eyes**,
for the father, my daddy has you right by his side.

Do not worry about **Mr. Exquisite** he will be OK,
for you know my daddy is the Potter and we are the clay,
his hands have crafted us to stand and to be strong,
For the hour coming where we will see you again, this I know
that it will not be long.

Save a spot for us while we handle work down here,
we will all see Jesus and rejoice together when we all get
there.

Psalms Of A Prophet

Subtitle: In The Midst of It All I got an Answer

So, Pamela (**Pretty Eyes**) we love you more than words can say,
today we celebrate your legacy in a special way,
by doing what you do best, by clocking in and going to work
right here and right now we going to bless God right here
today.

Is That All You See In Me?

If when you see me and I am not walking right,
Pray for me and bring me up to Jesus, not start a fight.

Why must when you look at me all you see is wrongness?
Have I not gone through enough and now I must feel less.

I often wonder do you hear or feel me.
Or better yet, do you even see me free?

Psalms Of A Prophet

Subtitle: In The Midst of It All I got an Answer

You look at me as though I am a disease,
And yet, do you find it hard to believe?

Father, I surrender to you,
The more I try the more I go through.

You said, "No weapon formed against me shall prosper," in your word,
But there are numerous of enemies revolting against me, that is what I heard.

You see me and yet you don't see me,
You hear what I say and yet ignore me you see,
And you say step back, I have the authority.

Who are you trying to prove yourself too?
To the one up above or to the one you are trying to bind to you like glue.

Vengeance is mine it belongs to me,
So, you better recognize who I am because in the end I will have won triumphally.

For I will stand for God despite all the things you do,
For greater is he that is in me, see I knew God was going to come through!

Psalms Of A Prophet

Subtitle: In The Midst of It All I got an Answer

Jesus Changed His Mind- 10/10/22.

Oh, I was in my feelings because Jesus changed his mind,
he saw how we were acting and said, "excuse me God, can you have some of your time?"

Jesus said, "dad, do you believe the nerve of this child of mine?"
out here slipping and sliding on my money and my dime!

They always want me to bless them and have their back,
but when I need them in return, they up in somebody's sack.

Can you imagine every time I come to their rescue, I pulled them out,
like dying on the cross wasn't good enough like they just get to walk about.

Son I already know your pain, didn't I say it repented me that I ever made man,
I was about to destroy the world you said father wait put their sins in the trash can.

But I am saying father I knew they had a heart for you,
guess I was wrong they're back to doing what they want to do.

Psalms Of A Prophet

Subtitle: In The Midst of It All I got an Answer

I guess I am the crazy one for getting beat, scorned, and pierced in my side for people I thought loved me,
but they chose to hop from bed to bed just for a one-minute quicky.

It's cool though I bet I won't get on the cross again for them,
If they are not careful, they will be in the lake of fire taking a swim.

Oh, daddy, can you believe what they just asked me to send them, a spouse!
But when I asked them for a prayer all I heard was crickets and a mouse.

Look there goes another one making their request be made known,
but when I asked them let's get in the word they pretend to act like drones.

Son this is not the time to be upset with them for you see you are on your way back soon,
just the faces of those that miss it, you know, like in the cartoons.

They will all remember your name on that day,
for it will be then and only then you get to have your way.

In the meantime, just hold your peace with these crazy ones,
It was you that went to hell snatching keys bringing back my sons.

Psalms Of A Prophet

Subtitle: In The Midst of It All I got an Answer

God can I just erase what I did at the cross?
So how many hearts feel so heavy I think I feel lost.

I know son I've been there a time or two,
But it was the love you gave that allowed them to get their breakthrough.

You see that right there look how they're worshiping you in spirit and in truth,
because of your sacrifice they get to honor you.

Don't change your mind on them just yet,
My plan for their lives has already been set.

My plan is to prosper them and make good on my plan,
for it is I that holds them in the palm of my hand.

So, son blessed those who despite fully use you,
It is the word you spoke to them on the very things to do.

So, son the question to you would you die for them all over again?
I would do it all over again so that they know you win!

Psalms Of A Prophet

Subtitle: In The Midst of It All I got an Answer

Just Who U R

For every tear you share represents hope,
For every frown on your face means that you cannot cope.

For every smile you share represents joy,
For every frustration in your life, it means its decoy.

Thinking in your mind that you are out there all alone,
Hear you say, "Please Lord hold my hand I am not made of stone".

For every thanks you give represents gratitude,
But for every thoughtless act means I have attitude.

Thinking about what it matters to anyone if I am here?
But a wonder comforter says child I am near.

I cannot take it I just don't have the ability,
Jesus said you're not listening because you have no stability.

My inner person has been wounded inside,
Like looking at broken pieces in a straight line.

I try to overcome this depression that I am in,
In my dark dreary spirit, I hear child you will not fit in.

Psalms Of A Prophet

Subtitle: In The Midst of It All I got an Answer

I made you different and unique in a very special way,
I put an empty void in you so that I may fill it one day.

You are my prize, fearful and wonderfully made,
Cast all your cares on me and at my feet all your burdens laid.

I care for you, my child; I bared it all so you may live,
Every pain I carried so that your life may be filled.

Dry your eyes and fly, fly high above your fears,
So, no worries my friends sing praise and get in gear,
For today you found the Comforter while He is near,
For today is your day so dry your tears,
So, no more worries I've cure all your fears.

Psalms Of A Prophet

Subtitle: In The Midst of It All I got an Answer

Last word from the author of Olivia Celestine

Whoa I am so glad to be out here they were working my nerves you see,
Everyone standing around fussing and caring over little on me.

They care for me until I took my last breath after I said my last piece,
Oh, Maysha you know he only gave me this body to lease.

I've buried some of my brothers, a son, and parents before I left this world to you,

Psalms Of A Prophet

Subtitle: In The Midst of It All I got an Answer

I know heaven has got a crown royal waiting and I am getting a new hairdo.

With my voice I have always instill that family are to pull together and love one another,
Now I know it's that Zachary blood it's like no other.

Be the glue that can never become undone,
Be better, be vibrant, be vigilant and put away the gun.

Remember we a legacy that loves to cook and show everyone how to get it done,
Oh, I remember I need someone to go to store gets some neck bones and cabbage we about to have some fun.

When I was younger, I gave them a run for their money,
Oh, my bad I am still making them run I am sweet like honey.

We come from that place of strength and passion and love,
Our love is so effective that it ascends upon you like a dove.

You are all nanny babies and the joy of my heart,
So, know that while I was here in every way, I did my part.

Don't be sad but continue to shine and do great things in this old earth,
They needed me in heaven to shake some things up not be here with all this dirt.

Psalms Of A Prophet

Subtitle: In The Midst of It All I got an Answer

Know that mommy, nanny, your sister loves you beyond measure
and feel my arms around you,
Just know as our last name mean God hath remember, so do I
too.

So, let's celebrate my babies y'all know that's exactly what I am
about to do.
Written: Derrick Zachary (nanny baby)

Left Your First Love

I remember when we use to commune with one another,
Now you have spent you r time with another lover,

You say you love me but really do you care?
I ask you to help others and their heavy load to share.

When you first dot with me you could not get enough of me,
Now I am trying to find you, can't get to you because you are moving
expedition ally.

Psalms Of A Prophet

Subtitle: In The Midst of It All I got an Answer

You used to take time out to see how I was doing,
Now you're spending time in your garden pruning.

You left me, why is that, may I ask?
Oh, excuse me! Was that just a hard task?

Nevertheless, I have some what an aught against thee,
You have left your first love; you are not committed to me.

You are so busy with the other things,
That if I came by to bless you, you could not receive anything.

You ask me to bless you tremendously,
But when I ask to pray, you could not get down on your knees to worship
me.

You cried, "Why is all hell breaking loose on me"?
Did you commune and talk to me, fall down, and say I surrender to thee.

Do you say, I already went through that process I'm not going through that
again?
You don't realize you left me, and you are filled with sin.

Me, filled with sin, I'm to holy for that,
You don't realize you have fallen off track.

Why can't you love that one that saved you?
Are the cares of the world more important to you?

You want to be on the forefront of the line,
When I ask you to come to me, I hear say I'm sorry I don't have time.

I love you; can't you see that?
Turn around child I don't want to see you back!

Psalms Of A Prophet

Subtitle: In The Midst of It All I got an Answer

I have an aught against you because you have left me,
Are we lovers, can we spend time together indefinitely?
Please don't tell me, you don't want me,
Cause I want you to have life eternally because I died for thee,
I just have one problem with you, why did you leave me?

MAINTIAN YOUR PRAISE

Psalms Of A Prophet

Subtitle: In The Midst of It All I got an Answer

Maintain your praise, in the midst of your suffering,

Maintain your praise, in the midst of your adversity.

The Lord knows where he is taking you,

Maintain your praise and let Him take you right on through.

Maintain your praise, in the midst of your afflictions,

Maintain your praise, in the midst of your persecutions.

For the Lord knows what he is doing for you,

Maintain your praise and walk right on through.

I know sometimes it seems unbearable, feel like you are going to lose your mind,

But a still small voice says, "I am always on time".

Maintain your praise in the midst of your pain,

I promise you; I will never let you go insane.

Psalms Of A Prophet

Subtitle: In The Midst of It All I got an Answer

Maintain your praise, no matter what you do,

But remember this before this world was form, I had already had a plan for you,

And that is I created praise deep down inside of you.

"MAKE THE VISION PLAIN"

It came when I was down and out,
A cloud of smoke surrounded me about.

In the smoke I heard a still small voice,
Be not afraid child it's not a choice.

I chose you to do a work to go forward and not back,
To be steadfast and not to fall off track.

The blood is required at your hand,
You haven't told my people of my plan.

I'm riding in a chariot of fire,
And is going to engulf them that are liars.

Make my vision plain for them that don't understand,
Not because they can't hear me, they just don't want the promised land.

The blood has been shed and there are rumors of wars,
My children have forsaken me and now stand behind bars.

But oh, that God would speak and open his lips against thee,

Psalms Of A Prophet

Subtitle: In The Midst of It All I got an Answer

Because you can't profess that you love me.

Have you not denied yourself yet?
Not so cause your life is filled with a lot of regrets.

Division has set in my people hearts!
Blood is being shed and you have yet to do your part.

You ask me, what do you want me to do?
But when I told you, you gave me the excuse that it is not you.

Write the vision and make it plain,
The handwriting on the wall and there is a famine in the land.

I have dried up your resources because you have not worshipped me,
And there will be no one to rescue thee.

I'm watching tears fall down from my daddy face,
Why did he issue out so much love on us and grace?

It repented him that he made you,
You have turned your back on him and now you don't know what to do!

I'm watching the angels in the throne room bow before the almighty,
And the enemy there stands around looking to see who he can take out immediately.

I saw him looking for me in the heavenly place,
But he could not touch me because of God grace.

He became angry because he could not have me,
He knew that god's love protected me.

I saw him looking for the elders to destroy them,
He could take the angels worshipping Elohim.

Psalms Of A Prophet

Subtitle: In The Midst of It All I got an Answer

He began to move round about the body worshippers of god,
I heard myself say, "Why me Lord"?

I was in a place that I had never been before,
A place where restoration was restored.

I heard the lord say, "have you considered my servant that loves me"?
Yeah, if I had my way, he would be bound not free.

My desire is to kill him and to destroy him,
But I can't because he belongs to you and my chances are slim.

What is so important about this little seed?
A seed created for praise that they may lead.

To lead a nation back to repentance to come back to me,
To be men and women walking in integrity.

So many of my people are living their lives in vain,
Putting them that live for me on the front line so their life may be slain.

If a brother or sister be naked and destitute of daily food,
You got to go down to the ghetto and take them out of the hood.

I saw the enemy disappear out of the holy place,
Watching Jesus love the next sinner with all of his grace.

I heard him say, "My child I chose you",
I chose you to be an example for them that are going through.

I died for you so that you may live,
I'll bless your life abundantly so that you may give.

Psalms Of A Prophet
Subtitle: In The Midst of It All I got an Answer

My Final Thoughts -10/6/21
In Memory of Renae Zachary

I am sweet, poised, and fine as wine,
that's how I attracted that man of mine.

You see I was in a place staying next in line for what God has for me,
that the man of mine looked past the outer and saw God's beauty inside of me.

It's not because I had the right words truth is I felt like no one cared for me,
but the father stepped in and said I have given you, my integrity.

Come take this journey with me as I take you on this ride of victory,
Yes, I know it may not seem like it but that's How I Met this, Zachary.

That boy Merrick was crazy for the Lord and full of life,
I was just trying to get to know him when I thought oh wow, he might be nice.

Little did I know one day the two of us would become one,
he was miracles in action, and I was river of life oh how did this crazy journey just begun.

He saw me when I did not see myself in that way,
he reminded me daily I love you from night until day,
don't you back down from the enemy this is what the Lord would say.

Psalms Of A Prophet

Subtitle: In The Midst of It All I got an Answer

I cried many nights from pain I was going through,
but that man of mine stepped in and showed me what to do.

Now you know the Zachary's can cook,
stayed in the kitchen preparing meals and reading a good book.

My grandkids are such characters that they have captured my heart,
sorry I had to leave you God needed me to do my part.

I'll cherish all my time with you,
but know this, there is nothing too hard for my God to do.

Don't cry dry those eyes I am still selling my paparazzi and my jewels for you,
taking orders, now Merrick get the wig you know what to do!

Y'all ever seen someone with so much energy and still finds time to cater to me,
now you can rest my love my dude Jesus and the crew they got me.

Continue to obey God in this season he has need of you,
Oh yes, just know I am still looking out for you.

My last words of love

Psalms Of A Prophet

Subtitle: In The Midst of It All I got an Answer

Dedicated to Kimberly (Gone to Early)

TO KNOW ME IS TO KNOW THE DEPTH OF ME,
THE KINDNESS OF MY NAME AND THE ROAR I CARRY IN THIS PLACE OF
VICTORY.

I SPENT TIME JUST TALKING TO THE FATHER ABOUT WHO I AM IN HIS
SIGHT,
LIKE THE I IN MY NAME THAT GAVE ME THE WILL TO FIGHT.

I UNDERSTOOD WHEN MY SAVIOR CALLED ME BY NAME,
HE SAID, "KIM COME FORTH NEVER HANG YOUR HEAD IN SHAME."

TO HAVE THE ABILITY TO BIRTH OUT TWO GREAT SONS THAT ARE
ORDAINED TO PREACH,
MY GREATEST JOY IS KNOWING HOW MANY SOULS THAT THEY SHALL
REACH.

WHO WOULD HAVE THOUGHT THAT THE CREATOR WOULD TAKE ALL MY
PAIN AWAY,
TODAY HEAVEN SMILED WHEN IT SHINES DOWN ON ME TODAY.

I WAS BROKEN INTO MANY PIECES BUT NEVER LETTING ANYONE SEE,
HAD TO REMIND MYSELF YOU ARE GREATER THAN YOUR PIECES, NOW
WALK IN YOUR VICTORY!

NEVER DID I GET TIRED OF PUSHING FOR THE BEST,
YOU KNOW ME, I TOLD EVERYONE IN THE CHURCH, THIS IS NOT THE TIME
TO REST.

I TAUGHT MY SONS NO MATTER WHAT NEVER GIVE UP,
GOD IS THE MENDER OF EVERY BROKEN CUP.

YES, I COULD HOLD THAT TENOR SECTION ON MY OWN,

Psalms Of A Prophet

Subtitle: In The Midst of It All I got an Answer

SO NOW I GET TO BOSS THESE ANGELS AROUND, HEY YOU STOP PLAYING
ON THE THRONE!

SEE THEY ALREADY TRYING ME, UP IN THESE HEAVENLY STREETS,
THEY DON'T KNOW ME LIKE THAT,
LET ME GET MY BAIL BONDSMAN ON AND BE LIKE JOE CLARK WITH MY
BAT.

WELL, I THOUGHT I WOULD LET YOU KNOW THAT I AM ALRIGHT UP HERE,
YOU ARE ALL GOING TO BE ALRIGHT PREACH THE WORD AND DON'T
WALK IN FEAR.

JUST KNOW MY LOVE SURROUNDS YOU EVERY DAY,
IT'S MY LAST WORDS TO YOU THAT GOD IS WITH YOU DAY BY DAY.

SO, I AM SHOUTING THE SONG, "WE HAVE THE VICTORY".
NOW RISE UP AND SQUARE YOUR SHOULDERS AND CONTINUE TO BE
FREE,
FOR MY GOD, HE HAS THEE...

My Legacy

Dedicated to Arthur Burkes

I never knew that it would end like this for me,
Who would have thought I shared a great legacy.

My words I spoke into others' lives,
Made them look way deep down on the inside.

Psalms Of A Prophet

Subtitle: In The Midst of It All I got an Answer

What made God choose a character like me,
Maybe it was because how I denied myself so that you
could the victory.

I was broken into many pieces but never letting anyone
see,
Told my children how daddy loved them and that they had
a great destiny.

Yes, my body did its thing,
But my father in heaven always carried me on his healing
wing.

Not ever did I get tired of pushing for the best,
My father said, come unto me and I will give you rest.

There were days I cried and cried and cried,
But I love me some Gwen who had me singing my my my my
my.

My legacy was to carry out the vision and to make it plain,
Came the Birthing out of Dry Bones Ministries, healing the
sick and the healing the lame.

Family has always been my focus,
Loving them was never any hocus pocus.

Psalms Of A Prophet

Subtitle: In The Midst of It All I got an Answer

I taught my sons no matter what never give up,
God is the mender of every broken cup.

I taught them to be kings and priests in the home,
To know that they will be great and never walk alone.

Taught my daughters that they are fearfully and
wonderfully made,
All wrapped in daddy arms, held close to his heart like
little babes.
Sure, I had my faults who hasn't these days,
But my praise and my worship said I can handle this come
what may.

Just know I am not in pain,
I didn't even feel like going insane.

He made me smile while I was going through,
The song, I won't complain, and praise is what I do, help me
make this journey to see the best in you.

So, I thank you for this great legacy you get to see,
That I got 2 wings, thank you God praise the lord I'm
free....

Psalms Of A Prophet

Subtitle: In The Midst of It All I got an Answer

Apostle Derrick Zachary
3/24/15

MY PROBLEMS

As my soul cry from all of the pain inside,
Would anybody choose to walk by my side.

The knives in my heart cannot compare to the love that it holds,
I realize that when chilly wind blows, I can withstand the cold.

I smile behind all the tears that I share,
Does anyone realize oh how much I can bare?

Excuses, excuses are all I ever hear,

Psalms Of A Prophet

Subtitle: In The Midst of It All I got an Answer

Blinded by their lust for sin they sit back and have a beer.

What happen to the ones that supposed to have your back,
They don't have time for me because they have fallen off track.

They mean well they really do,
But when you sit back and watch you know that they won't be there for you.

Made so many mistakes in my life,
But none can compare to all my sacrifice.

I gave and they take,
Watch the ones that said, "that they are my friend but end up being a snake."

If God be for you then its more than the world against you.
Can you help me push through?

I know in reality it's not your task,
But how long will you hide behind the mask.

I never seem to know who you are,
All I know it that you would rather sit at the bar.

I laugh at the hurt that I try to hide,
It could just be helping everyone and hiding my pride.

They walk by I know I see the need,
But they would rather hold their hands out and expect to always receive.

I have poured out everything in me,
Blood just oozing out, can anyone see?
I have beat myself up blaming myself for all of this pain,
When will just one person be there and hold my hand to keep me from going insane?

Psalms Of A Prophet

Subtitle: In The Midst of It All I got an Answer

My Vows

My spirit was quickening when I heard about you,
Knowing that you would be my rescuer that would bring me through.

The thought of it, I was chosen to be the one,
Not knowing that you prayed for the battle to be won.

Won in the spiritual realm where we got close,
But I had to pray also and stay on my post.

I' m crying because you chose me,
Not even knowing what kind of man I would turn out to be.

I cried for you daily and almost gave up,
But you told me I chose you because you saw a golden cup.

A cup that was once tarnishing and no good for anything,
But you saw beneath, behind, and in and turn it to something.

For that I chose you to be my bride,
To walk with me right by my side.

My vow to you is to cherish the gift you gave me,
A gift from you to me to be one in the heavenlies.

My vow is to protect you with everything that I got,
So, the enemy can't get in one little slot.

My vow is to love you unconditionally,
The love you sacrificed for me was to bring me next to thee.

Psalms Of A Prophet

Subtitle: In The Midst of It All I got an Answer

My vow is to respect you and to always desire you,
To make all your prayers and vision come true,
My vow is to just love you!

My Will or Yours –

2/21/14

Determined to excel in all that I do,
I decided to trust the master that created you.

Determined to prosper in everything meant for me,
You look and laugh but I am walking in my destiny.

I bowed down to you long enough,
I was developed with strength already made to be tough.

I saw you with the knife in your hand,
But before you got to me your life was like quicksand.

The stumbling block that you set in my way,
Made you trip up on the same day.

I called for help realizing no one could be there,
But a hand reached out to me, and I will never put more on you than
you can bear.

Psalms Of A Prophet

Subtitle: In The Midst of It All I got an Answer

There were rumors of lies that was said concerning me,
But God said don't retaliate you shall the victory.

My heart beating fast, pulse is racing ready to attack,
But the angel of the Lord taps me on the shoulder and said I got your back.

If they trespass against the you forgive them with all your heart,
If you choose the lesser you will not have done your part.

I made it through that test,
But I realize that my life is still a mess.

Merciful father I need you like never before,
These little issues can cause the closing of a door.

I command my spirit to rise above myself,
to be able to hear from whence cometh all my help.

I called you to be better than what you are,
You cannot live in church and in the bar.

Who is man that he would stand alone,
them that are perverted in their mind that have come and gone.

Stop procrastinating and do my will,
come out of the valley and be a light on top of a hill.

For you have played long enough,
for you pretend to be all that but you are not that tough.

Step out be who you are in me,

Psalms Of A Prophet

Subtitle: In The Midst of It All I got an Answer

get up it's time to stop acting like a tragedy.

Spirits have been released and they are after you,
So, I say what are you going to do?

Is it going to be my will or yours?
Choose life and live or choose death with every closing of doors.
And you will go from being rich to being poor.

Peculiar People, Peculiar Praise, Peculiar Promise

In a land a birth out a peculiar nation,

Psalms Of A Prophet

Subtitle: In The Midst of It All I got an Answer

A nation of praises of fasting and supplication.

I heard the land cry out to me,
A cry of a nation that desires to be free.

But in their freedom, they have gotten slack on me,
Not giving me glory and not shouting for the victory.

In a land there is one that stands alone,
Crying for the people that have left me and doing things on their own.

They have committed adultery against me,
My nation is dying, can't you see?

I raised you up to proclaim my name,
And yet you had chosen to remain the same.

I told you; I chase whom I love,
But you are attached to sin like a ball to a glove.

What would it take for you to surrender all?
I'm taking my hedge off you, and you shall fall.

See being peculiar requires you to be different from the world,
And you are drawn to the life of fake pearls.

I need a voice to stand up against the enemy,
Not a bunch of half-stepping people who think they have plenty.

A promise I made between you and I,
But you're watching too much stuff with your evil eyes.

Oh, children I see bloodshed in the land,

Psalms Of A Prophet

Subtitle: In The Midst of It All I got an Answer

Building your houses on sinking sand.

You told me not my will but yours be done,
Yet you drop the word of God to pick up a gun.

Have I not delivered you time after time?
Yet I ask you to worship me and you say nothing like a mime.

I promised you I would never leave you nor forsake you,
And you want me to bless you, and you can't go through.

Wait, I hear something in my ear,
A voice crying out for the people, this must be the year.

The year my people has surrender all,
A transformation from Saul to Paul.

I see my people blessing me,
They change their lives and walking in victory.

My peculiar people have return to me,
My angels are rejoicing that they are free.

Go forth my people and tell of my goodness,
Tell them that don't know about my son name Jesus.

Oh, I hear you rejoicing and shouting for joy,
I see my people being delivered from all decoys.

I see you taped into the vision that I have set before thee,
My sons and daughters are now walking in liberty,
This is what pleases me,
My children blessing, worshipping, and dancing in victory,

Psalms Of A Prophet

Subtitle: In The Midst of It All I got an Answer

That is what pleases me.

Rejected Because I Don't Know You - 2/13/11.

Father, I know you must be angry with all the mess that is
going on,
I know that I am, how much more can this pain be prolonged?

I see the tears falling rapidly down from your face,

Psalms Of A Prophet

Subtitle: In The Midst of It All I got an Answer

here daddy take my shawl and wipe your tears and tell me about the case.

Child, I have no more grace to give out to these rebellion ones,
Why have they lost trust in me and now they're picking up guns.

Now I am angry at the children of disobedience for playing with me,
They are liars, cheaters, deceivers and walking after their own beat.

How can you expect for me to bless them in all their mess,
Yet they gripe and complain and call themselves blessed.

They don't even realize that it is the enemy that tricked them into thinking they can continue that way,
I have taken my hands off them because destruction shall be their end of day.

In the dungeon trying to speak a word,
God said it is my voice you've heard.

The Thunder is loud, and the lightning is flashing,
but today my people you will get a good lashing!

My hand wasn't too short that I could not save you on my ear
so heavy that I could not hear you,

Psalms Of A Prophet

Subtitle: In The Midst of It All I got an Answer

the sin I cannot look upon especially because it is in you.

Yes, you can cry and say Lord you know my heart,
I don't know it well and yet it is sin in you that does its part.

Hello, can you continue to act like you don't care for me?
I see corruption on top of corruption and death shall be your
destiny.

I am riding my Chariots of horses from heaven to get my
chosen ones,
oh, you know the ones you talked about that you said they look
like bums.

Yeah, they were my vessels willing to be used,
I wanted to use you, but you were a ticking time bomb without
a fuse.

Oh, I heard the language that came from your lips,
standing there bold in my presence with your hands on your hips.

I used to trust you to go forth and declare my word,
now you are just an adjective not even an adverb.

Prayer is no longer in your vocabulary skills,
all you want to do is get even and kill, kill, kill.

Now it's my turn to show you who I am,

Psalms Of A Prophet

Subtitle: In The Midst of It All I got an Answer

for the great judgment book is open and it's not Uncle Sam.

This book represents the names that are written for my glory, oops I'm so sorry you might want to find another book to tell your story.

Don't see your name in this lamb book of life, have to close this one and open death and hell book where your name might be next to strife.

So many names just give me a minute to search for your name, oh, there it is right there next to guilt and shame and the blame game.

I need you to step aside and let my little ones that suffer for me to come through, Your gate is 4 doors down, goodbye, and good luck to you.

I tried to save them all but hey what can you do? I told you to get out of this line, this area does not belong to you!

Don't pay attention to all this screaming going on down there, They are just doing the dance called the burning layer.

Preachers, teachers, apostles, murderers, liars, pimps, and players are all waiting on you,

Psalms Of A Prophet

Subtitle: In The Midst of It All I got an Answer

They told me that you were the head ringleader that could get the joint hop in with the throwback dew.

I have warned and worn and now I am through dealing with you,
cannot save you anymore there is no more intercession for you.

I hope you have fun they are doing all the latest craze,
Come on my little child, I heard you were brave.

you faced life to the fullness just to see my glory,
Today the angels in heaven will begin to tell your story.

You made it into the mansion that I wrote your name upon title he won,
here is a ring and A roll because you were the chosen one.

Overcomer shall be your name throughout the earth,
no more crying being sick from nothing but hurt.

Welcome in my good and faithful servant for going all the way,
today I say I love you in the biggest way,
Welcoming you home and celebrating your day.

God smiled at me with a gleam in his eye,
wrapped me in his arms and sang me the sweetest lullaby.

For I knew he was well pleased with me,

Psalms Of A Prophet
Subtitle: In The Midst of It All I got an Answer

but I wonder did the others make it into this peaceful heavenly?

REVELATION

It seems like we have lost our way,
Can we sit and talk about it today?

Remember when I used to be first in your life?
Ask yourself when the last time was you made a sacrifice.

Remember when I was all that you needed?
Now I'm on the throne with God begging and pleading.

Remember when you used to be in love with me?
Remember when you used to dance for me?

It seems like it doesn't exist anymore.
Now you are in the middle of a battle with the pity pat of life's gore.

Eternity with me used to be on your mind.
Now you are in and out waiting for a sign.

You went around helping those that were down and out.
Now it's about what you want, and you are standing in doubt.

You used to sing to me late at night.
Can I ask you a question? Where is the fight?

Psalms Of A Prophet

Subtitle: In The Midst of It All I got an Answer

No matter what came your way, you would stand.
Now your brother and sister have fallen, and you won't give a
helping hand.

You criticized those that try to make a change.
Does it bother you that that might seem strange?

We are speaking the word, and it goes up in the air.
But we sit up in church while we play with our hair.

I used to be your lifestyle every day.
I can't get you to even bless me today.

You used to respect each other when someone walked by.
Ask yourself, "are you willing to die?"

I am rising up a nation that will stand through anything.
Not bow to the enemy, not caught up with the bling.

A generation that would love me,
To spend time with each other continuously.
One that is not scared of giving me praise.
Someone not scared to stand on the front line and be brave.

I refuse to lose a battle that is already promised to be won.
Can you get with the program? You are the chosen one!

The battle you will have to face is like one never before.
Hold on children for it is I standing and knocking at the door.

Psalms Of A Prophet

Subtitle: In The Midst of It All I got an Answer

I am knocking because I want you to know I am with you.
For I have given you the Revelation. What are you going to do?

Seek To Find Me

Life as we know it may not be the same,
But if we trust in God, we can realize there is power in his name.

Psalms Of A Prophet

Subtitle: In The Midst of It All I got an Answer

Life in this world we can easily get caught up in,
To please the world in a world of sin.

To see the real you is hard to identified,
Except, when you realize who it was who died.

To be mysterious in a way to please others,
We can prolong longer, and we'll back up farther and further.

To admire without touching the outer you,
To want to touch but not executing you through.

To capture your inner glow is their plan,
But you realize that God has the upper hand.

They wanted to destroy your body, mind, and soul,
But in order to do that they must get permission from God; he has made you whole.

They mean to harm you,
But to capture you they must find out the depth of you, oh my what to do?

The beauty that shines out through you is so hard to be around,
I am honored that it was I the love that I found.

Be still and wait for an endless enduring love that won't past,
As long as you stay focused you can last.

Tough and hard as you try to be,
It is I the one lover that you ask for you see.

All that you have prayed for is in me,
But to have me you must be free,
Well now that I have your attention is it I, yet you seek?

Psalms Of A Prophet

Subtitle: In The Midst of It All I got an Answer

SOUL SEARCHER

Blinded by the memories in my mind,
That I kept all bad and left out all the kind.

Frighten day by day that I'm going to fall,
Yes, I know sometimes we must a hit wall.

Lay awake at night tossing and turning in the bed of pain,
Trying to keep myself from going insane.

I find myself running and running to a place called, NO where,
A place called sorrow, hey have you been there?

Feel like I'm in a maze searching for a way out,
Face by many obstacles standing their face about.

Head hurts, eyes swollen, heart so heavy,
Feels like all of me is standing on a very edgy levy.

Sure, I wear a smile to hide the tragedies in my life,
But you know what; it is me, not anyone else that made the
ultimate sacrifice!

I give and give, and they take and take until there is no more,
I ran and hid and cried, dust myself off and run to the next
door.

Psalms Of A Prophet

Subtitle: In The Midst of It All I got an Answer

A pain, a cry, a hurt, that feels the air,
I wonder have anybody else been there?

Still I Overcame

You see you laughed, called me out my name,

Jesus said, "Yes child still I overcame".

You went around spreading your rumors and your lies,

Took me by a storm because I thought you were a friend of mine.

You thought you were better than everyone around you,

Psalms Of A Prophet

Subtitle: In The Midst of It All I got an Answer

You made a fool out of your own self when you do what you do.

You smile in my face pretending like everything is fine,

But all along you were trying to put a knife in my spine.

The sign on you says beware of false person trying to harm you,

Jesus said, "Still I overcame so no danger would come to you".

Looking like a snake not harmless at all,

But very venomous waiting to strike at every beacon call.

Laugh if you must and spread your lies,

In the end I still overcame, and your soul might die.

Psalms Of A Prophet
Subtitle: In The Midst of It All I got an Answer

The Appreciation of Love
Dedicated to Apostle Mario Davis

Could not understand the journey I was on until I met this brother,
He spoke words of wisdom like no other.

The kindness that blows out of him encourage me to go on,
To hear the songs of old, oh to be kept by Jesus and leaning on his
everlasting arms.

The days he sacrificed for others to be great in his sight,
Proves himself over the years that he can handle any fight.

I've seen him cry and I've seen him sad,
But with one-word Jesus, it made him glad.

Ever wonder why he kept pushing you, because his heart desire is to
see the best operate in you.

Never allowing you to abort your mission in life,
Mario learns to love you beyond you without getting into all the
strife.

He traveled to make sure that I was OK when I was sick,
Told the devil back up off of him, I know your trick.

Even when he felt like giving it all up,
Listen I prophesied to you that God is refilling your cup.

For you have much work to do in this day,
That every stream of blessing is about to flow your way.

Psalms Of A Prophet

Subtitle: In The Midst of It All I got an Answer

For God has seen the tears you shed,
He has even seen the times your heart has blessed.

But know this God, Jesus, and the Holy Ghost is on your side,
What he is about to download to you will come by surprise.

Look before you, the rain is coming to shower you,
for your not Second thought but I am bringing a wind of miracles to
overshadow you.

Be encouraged this day because we are here to celebrate you,
And God the father says I honor you.

The Champion

The champion has arrived, can you see him?
He is fighting on your side so don't you fear them.

I have your back covered is what you told me,
Today is your sentence devil for I have the victory.

I must go through things in order to gain faith,
To persist and pursue and to lay aside every weight.

The more I react to the things of the flesh I haven't learned the
lesson that I need to learn,
For when I've learned it, I will realize that there are greater blessings
to be earned.

Psalms Of A Prophet

Subtitle: In The Midst of It All I got an Answer

Battles come so I can stand up against to win,
Not bow to the flesh and sin!

The champion has arrived, can you feel him?
A sure way of winning is don't fear them!

Excuse me while I praise God for the victory, he has given to me,
To persist, pursue, and overtake do you see what I see?

Heartaches and pain yes, they will come,
But keep your hands in the master's hands and there will be a bigger
sum.

Wipe those tears from those precious eyes,
It is I the champion who has come to revive.

Stand tall and know who you are my child,
Quit going back to the world to come back wild.

There is nothing in Egypt so leave Egypt there,
It is I the champion who fought the fight to show you I care.

The champion has arrived do you see him,
Step back Satan, my big brother Jesus has slain them!

The Chosen- 7/2/23

Psalms Of A Prophet

Subtitle: In The Midst of It All I got an Answer

Just to know that you are chosen from your mother's womb,
some would say your life is already doomed.

He had crafted me with the ability to see,
the sight to see every ability in me.

He crafted me after his own heart,
God build a bridge for me so that I always have a place to avoid the darts.

He looked at me and smiled with such a gleam in his eyes,
All I could do was to worship and to transcend my love to the skies.

I gather that these moments became intimate you see,
just the essence of the beauty between him and me.

Of course, I tried to run away from him,
but he had the angels slow walk me down and say, "what are you trying to
do slim?"

I really thought I could escape the path he had sent for me,
Listen, he just doesn't choose you for an assignment he hadn't already
given you the victory.

One component is the mantle of his DNA he places on you,
like a whole home and tracking that turns around and locates you.

I believe he just looked for the one that has his spark,
not the one that say they at church but when they really are at the park.

Hey, you guess what there are some wonderful perks,
but in retrospect you must look out for the ones that act like jerks.

Are you capable of handling being chosen?
but there are few requirements though don't end up like the movie frozen.

Psalms Of A Prophet

Subtitle: In The Midst of It All I got an Answer

Once your mind understands you'll be just fine,
but just don't stand there acting like a mime.

Who among you is the chosen one,
Could you recognize it are you too busy having fun?

At any moment God cashes in on his chosen people out there,
When he does, don't come with options; you know like choosing meat, oh I
like mine medium rare.

God designed you to be chosen because he had need of you,
chosen or not what are you going to do?

The Night Before- 3/1/22

Twas the night before Jesus and all through the house,
I heard silence in the air, no one praying, not even the spouse.

Children were creeping out the window with no care,
while mom was crying in the bedroom saying, "Lord how much
more do I have to bear"?

Dad is passed out drunk after he just stopped beating his wife,
Wow, the sun is standing in the hallway with a big butcher
knife.

Thoughts in the son mind and he calls himself a man of God
and a great preacher,

Psalms Of A Prophet

Subtitle: In The Midst of It All I got an Answer

if this is the God, he serves then I will let the devil be my teacher.

My spirit is grieved from what I was looking at tonight,
How can this be your servant that professes you but does not represent the light.

As I leave, I entered another house that has caught my eye,
As I entered this place, boy was I in for a surprise.

Is that the deacon with one of the members of the church?
Is his hand on her thighs now moving up her skirt?

She began to tell him stop I cannot do this we are saved,
his reply it's OK it's the latest crave!

She's trying to escape from him she said, "No!"
but he forces himself on her and said, "for it shall be so."

I cannot believe my eyes at what I see,
Am I being tricked, or do my eyes deceive me?

The father says oh just wait at what's coming up,
dry your eyes for you must see it here take a sip from my cup.

As I am led by the father he brings me to the church door,
well at least here I know the word is preached right down to the core.

Psalms Of A Prophet

Subtitle: In The Midst of It All I got an Answer

Hey son let's go in to see if you are right,
We entered the sanctuary wait, are they about to fight?

Are they cussing from the pulpit, is this what we do?
Listen father I am over all of this is this what it has come
to?

I need someone to see what I see every day,
now I need a John the Baptist to rise up and prepare the
way.
For you see I am on my way back and many shall be lost,
many are preaching and they have not counted up the cost.

I need your voice to be loud in the earth,
to deal with the forms of godliness and to deal with the dirt.

More in them for I have seen their sins for it is great and has
come up before me,
destruction is coming for those who use their platform for
treachery.

I am starting with these leaders who have used my name in
vain,
for they will be the one like the sheep that was led to be slain.

Tell them for every word they profess I said,
Today I had the father have dried up their fame.

Psalms Of A Prophet

Subtitle: In The Midst of It All I got an Answer

Tell them their dirty laundry shall be exposed to the one I
chose to be revealed,
tell them that it's not the show let's make a deal.

Prepare the way for I'm coming back,
question have you followed it directions or did you fall off
track?

The Other Side of Through

Stumbling and fumbling around in the dark can someone help me,
I have been trying to find my way, but I cannot see.

I hear voice calling out to me, "I need you",
What is it exactly that they want, can I get through?

I hear them say come back to me,
Everyone is pulling me in a direction I don't want to be.

The further I go up the more they call,
I've seen others get to where I am and fall.

But there is a goal that I am trying to reach,
Can you help me get there or will you be a leech?

I hear a voice say keep striving on,
For there is a greater reward for them that diligently press on.

Tears roll down from all the frustration and chaos in my life,
But my focus and style are to stay on that narrow track.

Psalms Of A Prophet

Subtitle: In The Midst of It All I got an Answer

Constantly I am dodging bullets and knives coming towards me,
I learn to maneuver to keep my sanity.

They call me cruel names, everything but a child of God,
But a word came unto me saying, "My child be strong".

Wipe your eyes and sing your way through,
For this is only a test to see what you would do.

They will try to break you if you let them,
But I have given you something greater to stand on the weakest limb.

So, dry your eyes my child I have your back,
For every promise I promise you it's already on the outpouring track.

Just jump upon the train and ride,
I'll continue to hold you in my arms and sing to you confronting la la byes.

For united we stand and divided we fall,
But when it's time will you hear the call.

Press my child to that goal that you have set,
And I guaranteed that God has never fell you yet.

I know sometimes you just don't know what to do,
But remember this there is a blessing on the other side of through!

THE PROCESS
4/28/10

Crinkly and rough looking I realize what I was,

Psalms Of A Prophet

Subtitle: In The Midst of It All I got an Answer

Proving to be sharp and polished, boy I feel like a just cause.

I hated the process of being peeled, I saw me,
It was disgusting and I thought I was ruining my destiny.

Have you ever been so broken that it seems that the pieces would never come together again?
But you look to the right, and you see a new life will begin.

Lest thou learn his ways and get a snare soul,
Could I be that important and can I be made whole?

The first layer to me was deceit that was I could see,
The next layer was me beating up on me.

There was no wisdom or understanding for the things I faced,
Nothing but a shattered broken body, which needed to be replaced.

I cried so loud that still no one heard me,
Could we be that into ourselves that we walk in cruelty?

One slap to the face and they say turn the other cheek,
When I'm ready to retaliate I heard a voice that said, "Son stay meek."

I bit my lip from trying not to explode,
Like all the soap operas, you are waiting for the next episode.

Had a gun to my head from people trying to still the inner peace in me,
Why would those perverted degenerated people ruin my beauty?

My tears have been my meat both day and night,
Mine enemies speak evil of me, when shall he die, do you think he can fight?

I speak of things which I have made touching the king,
This process is unbearable in the worst way, that every day I am dying.

When I remember these things, I pour out of my soul in me,
For thy art the God of my strength and all my ability.

Psalms Of A Prophet

Subtitle: In The Midst of It All I got an Answer

Here I am oh God with my hands out stretch to thee,
You created something wonderful in me,
It's all because of the process called the winner in me.

The Revolution

My brothers and sisters, have you ever been fed up with mess?
Then you find yourself praying that someone else would be blessed.

My brothers and sisters, have you ever been in a place where you felt like losing your mind?
Then the Lord stepped in right on time.

My brothers and sisters, have there ever been somebody that has worked your nerves?
But you knew if you gave up, the blessing you would miss around the curve.

My brothers and sisters, aren't you sick of people playing games?
Trying to show off for one day of glory and fame.

My brothers and sisters, aren't you tired of trying to search for love?
When the Lord said, "If you run to my arms, I will be your heavenly dove."

My brothers and sisters, are you tired of people lying to you?
For once in their life that they would tell the truth.

My brothers and sisters, aren't you tired of running away?
The Lord said if you serve me, I will bless you today.

My brothers and sisters, why don't you encourage each other?
Or is it so much better hating one another?

My brothers take a stand and be the man God has called you to be,
My sisters stop putting down yourselves and see what God see.

My brothers would you stop putting your hands on God precious ones,
My sisters would you stop putting down who God is trying to raise up.

My brothers and sisters know who you are and what you can be,

Psalms Of A Prophet

Subtitle: In The Midst of It All I got an Answer

You are the peculiar, uncommon, and holy priest the ones God has raised up to set the world free.

My brothers and sisters have you ever said, "How much more do I have to take?"
Then you search inside yourself and realize that God had sealed your faith.

Get tired of all the worries that you carried from day to day,
God said, "Here am I child, here to make away."

Run to my arms and I will carry you,
The weight of the world has oppressed you.

Is it worth carrying mess on your shoulders and your heart?
Let me come in and do my part,
I will reveal to you the mysteries in my heart.

Run to my arms my daughters and sons,
I died for you so that your battles will be won.

THE SOUND

IT CAME TO PASS THAT A SOUND CAME TO MY EAR,
WAS ANY ONE PAYING ATTENTION DO THEY HEAR WHAT I HEAR?

THE SOUND WAS SO LOUD THAT GOD SAID DON'T BE IN DESPAIR,
I HEAR HIM SAYING THE REMNANT I CAM TO REPAIR.

MY CHOSEN I HAVE HEARD YOU AND I CAME TO BUILD YOU UP,
I SAW THAT YOU WERE BROKEN BUT I CAME TO FILL YOUR CUP.

THE ENEMY DESIRE TO TAKE YOU OUT,

Psalms Of A Prophet

Subtitle: In The Midst of It All I got an Answer

I AM THE PROTECTOR OF YOUR SOUL NOW GIVE ME A SHOUT.

I PUT A HEDGE AROUND SO NOTHING CAN HARM YOU,
I AM THE KING OF KINGS, I KNIGHT YOU WITH OIL OF WORSHIP SO I
ANOINTED YOU.

I HID YOU FROM THE FACE OF THE ONE THAT SEEKS YOU OUT,
AND YET YOU ARE STANDING THERE LIKE YOU HAVE GOUT.

I COVERED YOU WITH MY HEALING WING,
CAN YOU NOT HEAR THE ANGELIC VOICE OF MY ANGELS SING.

ARISE SOLIDER ITS TIME TO SQUARE YOUR SHOULDERS AND PLANT YOUR
FEET,
IT'S TIME YOU HEAR THE SOUND AND WALK TO MY BEAT.

THERE IS A WAR GOING ON BETWEEN THE EVIL ONE AND THE SAINT,
THIS IS NOT THE TIME FOR YOU TO STAND AND COMPLAIN, JUST MAKE
SURE THAT YOU DO NOT FAINT.

HEAR YE THE SOUND ITS LOUD AND CLEAR,
KNOW THAT THE SAVIOUR THE REDEEMER IS NEAR,
SO, WALK IN ME WITH CONFIDENCE AND DO NOT FEAR,
FOR I THE SAVIOR IS VERY CLOSE AND NEAR.

The Time

1-12-2012

The time of trouble is what you foreseen to come,
a time of refreshing and restoration for the weak and the dumb.

At times of being broken and shattered is what you were looking to happen to you,
but I said behold, be healed, is what I already designed for you.

The time of separation almost was unbearable for you to take,
But know, what I was designing in you wasn't by any means a mistake!

At one time you thought there would be no more tears from so much you had already shed,
but each one was uniquely designed, so that your soul may be fed.

The times your heart was breaking into so many little pieces from all the attacks,
but not one time did ever not have your back.

You've done so much for everyone never receiving anything in return,
instead, they fed you lies and watch you just get burned.

In this time, I was making you into something indestructible for my glory,

Psalms Of A Prophet

Subtitle: In The Midst of It All I got an Answer

because I could only trust you to tell my story.

The things you went through was designed to try to turn you against me,
but you didn't allow it to affect the relationship between you and me and your destiny.

I knew you felt so alone in those darkest of nights,
but you reminded everyone that even in the darkest hour, God is a shining light.

I am a rewarding you now for everything you have endured,
because when others saw You to be weak, I saw you as being matured.

You won't have to say a word to anyone they will see,
that for being faithful to me I am rewarding you openly.

They will walk right up to you and bless you and they can't say anything,
For my favor is upon you and I am carrying healing in my wing.

I have elevated you and prepared a table in the presence of your enemy,
You will not be afraid, but you will speak with the authority of the Trinity.

For it is your time to shine bright in this season,
not to be brought up on charges and sentence for false treasons.
It is I God almighty that has his hands on you,
There is nothing no one can say or even do, because it's your time to come right on through.

Psalms Of A Prophet

Subtitle: In The Midst of It All I got an Answer

The Tomb 5/5/13

My tune turned into my womb it caused me to produce greater,
It has sustained me from such a time as this to be a producer in
this season.

Psalms Of A Prophet

Subtitle: In The Midst of It All I got an Answer

In this tomb it was dark and damp,
But I heard a voice that said will you be my lamp?

Can you shine even though you are in your darkest moment right
now,
For I am raising standards all over town.

You have entertained the world and the pleasures of sin,
Do you not know that you can win?

I carried you in my heart,
but the enemy tries to tear you apart.

You've had restless nights ready to die,
but my spirit spoke to you and said get untied.

You laid here long enough in your mess,
for I your father have called you to be blessed.

The rats have been watching where you go,
The wolves sniffed you out while you were low.

The snakes have latched on to your hand,
They already knew that you had an anointing to possess the land.

You must get out of this grave,
Your time is up. I am here to fill your cup you are no longer a
slave.

I called you out of where you were comfortable at,
for I am sending the angels of war to have your back.

Psalms Of A Prophet
Subtitle: In The Midst of It All I got an Answer

Walk this way for the world have not seen what I'm about to do, for you will possess a power that will show up just for you.

<u>The Unfinished Prophetic Word- 5/15/17</u>

The anointing you are caring isn't just for you,
but it will bring you to the captives to bring them all the way through.

The process was to make you better than you've ever been before,
when you dealt with life's little hiccups and its gore.

They could not write your story it was never meant for them,
but your testimony will bring you before the lost and the dim.

The broken will experience the glory of who I am,
you will not be enlisted or drafted into Uncle Sam.

I have brought you to the brooks,
I have given you a great blessing and a great hook.

This hook is going to cause men to pour into you,
My next manifestation is going to shift all of you.

Psalms Of A Prophet

Subtitle: In The Midst of It All I got an Answer

All the tears you've been crying I am drying them up,
for at the table that I have prepared, I am about to fill your
cup.

Death has been trying to take you out,
but my angels are on standby ready to give a shout.

Stand still and see the salvation of the Lord it shall work for
you,
but my hands were upon you to be the vessel I use to complete
the work you do.

But I put a cloud over your head,
but it is I the only one that 5000 I fed.

Lean not to your own understanding for it never works,
but continue to live in me and you shall receive all the perks.

The Untouchable One-
10/14/23

Gather round get a little closer let me tell you about this one,
the nerves of the people that tried to break you, but they haven't won.

You see from birth you were already different and wise,
They said this one will stand alone and be despised.

Psalms Of A Prophet

Subtitle: In The Midst of It All I got an Answer

Unique in your worship capture the attention of many around you,
but many are seeking to figure you out too.

The times have been equaled against you since you been in this world,
but grace with power to stand you didn't bow or twirl.

You achieve the impossible that others could not do,
The glow that you show makes your anointing come through.

The enemy tried to ruin your godly name,
one thing I realized not one time did you hang your head in shame.

Brilliantly you are skilled with words too shut the enemy up,
I've watched you be empty, and the Lord shows up to fill your cup.

Pressing through the storms that could have taken you out,
but I watched the angels come to your rescue just to pull you out.

I heard the Lord say, "that you will speak to the great kings in the land",
You never allow the influence of the crowd get you in the quicksand.

Life is fulfilled with simple joys and blessings without end,
You never allow the joys of the world get you wrapped up in sin.

You see, God has need of you,
Only you can release an oil that would bring this world through.

You carry a legacy from generations before you,
Except they were called to it, but you were chosen to carry what others could not
do.

Remember God has never let you down,
He has held you, wiped your tears, and turn your frown into a beautiful sound.

No one else could do what you do,
It's because the father really loves him some of you.

Psalms Of A Prophet

Subtitle: In The Midst of It All I got an Answer

THE WORTHY LAMB

THERE WAS A LAMB THAT WAS SLAIN.

HE DIDN'T KNOW WHY, BUT HE KNEW THE WORLD HE MUST GAIN.

OH GOD! IT DIDN'T HURT FOR HE MUMBLES NOT A WORD,

OH, IF IT WAS ME COULD I BE TREATED LIKE A HERD.

AN INNOCENT PURE LITTLE LAMB,

SEEMS LIKE HE WAS ALWAYS IN A JAM.

BUT BECAUSE THAT LAMB KNEW HIS JOB,

THE PEOPLE GOT MAD AND BECAME A VICIOUS MOB.

MY HEARTACHE WHEN I THINK I COULD HAVE HELPED THAT POOR SOUL,

BUT BECAUSE HE SAID, "NO I MUST BARE THIS ALONE!"

Psalms Of A Prophet
Subtitle: In The Midst of It All I got an Answer

IT HURT ME SO BADLY THAT I COULD NOT HELP,

BUT HE PAID THE PRICE FOR YOU AND ME, HE SAID;
"NOW YOU CAN HELP YOURSELF".

WORTHY IS THAT LAMB THAT WAS SLAIN YOU SEE,

IF IT HAD NOT BEEN FOR THAT LAMB, WOULD
ANYTHING BE?

These Streets and These Houses- 1/12/12

This journey that I was on was one that I didn't understand,
 All I kept hearing was I am upholding you with my right hand.

I felt at peace about it but was curious why me,
I was so low and broken that I felt like nothing but a hollow tree.

I'm walking by people that cannot even see me,
Am I that invisible that no one sees the depth of me?

I travelled down the road a little further and came to a White House,

Psalms Of A Prophet

Subtitle: In The Midst of It All I got an Answer

I didn't hear anything moving, not even a mouse!

It felt cold and no love was in there,
The sign on the House said, how much more can you bear?

This question was powerful for I was already at the end of my rope,
but a member of the house came out dressed in a robe and said to me
keep moving for there is no hope.

The words caught me off guard, so I stepped down with my head
hung low,
I looked up and the house across the street had a sign that said, you
can't enter if you are not willing to sow.

I had nothing to give or offer there it seems that it was all about a
show,
I was in search of an answer to help me get back into the flow.

As I continue to walk down the road another house that was inviting
me in,
but as a stranger came by and said if you go in you will definitely be
in sin.

The house seemed to have everything I need for this time,
but everyone's face was painted, you know, they look like mimes.

No one seemed real, they all seemed fake,
What was that I saw a spirit moved in that house it took look like a
snake.

I ran from that place clearly it wasn't right for me,
God, can they not see what I see!

Psalms Of A Prophet

Subtitle: In The Midst of It All I got an Answer

The next place was set right in the middle of a graveyard with a sign
that says, "we want you",
maybe I would be off better there I was already empty hmm what
should I do?

A stranger came to me and said that is not what God promised you,
pass this place, death was never designed for you.

Why was it so easy for others to do wrong,
why did I have to go through loneliness, raped, beating, and still
must be strong,
God, can you not hear me how long?

It seemed like it was empty words that was just uttered,
I felt so low, solo that I felt like I was in the gutter.

But keep moving something just wouldn't let me give up,
a stranger came by again and said for your pain here is a golden cup.

I didn't understand why I had this cup in my hand,
but the spirit said unto me, child I need you to stand.

I continue to press my way despite what I was feeling,
I realized that every step I took the enemy was getting scared, so he
went to Whaling and dealing.

As I move, I look to my left and saw a glass house,
The house was so dirty but to everyone they said you and dirt it was
the pronounce.

I couldn't understand how they could judge everyone about their sin,

Psalms Of A Prophet

Subtitle: In The Midst of It All I got an Answer

but a house that is so filthy clearly didn't want anyone in.

I have walked in a way that was unknown to man,
but the spirit was leading me into this sinful land.

Every route that I took did not make sense to me,
but God said to me be still and know that you will walk in victory.

Ever wondered what the streets had to offer for you,
clearly, I did too but I'm just walking trying to make it through.

As I continue walking up this street there was this house that I came
upon that you could tell that there was peace there,
Could this be the place for me because I just don't know how much
more I could bear!

They welcomed me in with open arms,
never ever feeling like anyone would do me harm.

They started singing this heavenly music that opened my ears,
before I knew it God had wiped all my fears.

I realized that if you just keep on moving and allowing God to lead
you,
The next place you may end up is right where you need to be so that
your life is brand new.

Together the Two Shall Become One

Psalms Of A Prophet

Subtitle: In The Midst of It All I got an Answer

Blending into a moment of a solitary thread,
the pulse of life merging into one they read.

Where the two have begun they release themselves and yield,
the spirit of the Lord showered down on them like rain falling in an
open field.

All the passion, all the of the fire, all they were and all they are,
all they would become and every tear they shared was put into a jar.

With their hopes, the desires, and their dreams,
Were blessings flowing like fish swimming in a stream.

To become lost to oneself and exist within the instant,
that comes between two heartbeats, my God they were persistent.

When at last the two, shall become one,
they walk after the trueness of God and not after weapons of the gun.

They were talked about for going forward with God's destiny,
but they decided to follow God from here until infinity.

no matter what came their way, they made a choice to stand,
Now your brothers and sisters have fallen, and they always show a
helping hand.

they speak words of encouragement, and it goes into the air,
but we sit up in church just looking, while we play with our hair.

The battle they will have to face it's like no one ever before,
hold on children for it is I standing and knocking at the door.

Psalms Of A Prophet

Subtitle: In The Midst of It All I got an Answer

I am knocking because I want you to know I am with you,
 for I have given you the revelation. What are you going to do?

Can you understand the pain that they are caring for me?
Does it bother you when they turn to the left or to the right there is
their enemy?

It bothers them that your sister turns to a man that hits her every
night,
And it bothers them to know if your brother will ever decide to walk
in the light!

Why did we turn away from what we know?
When God says, "come to me and I'll wash you whiter than snow."

 they knew eventually you would turn back to me,
 in the midst of all I have an answer for thee,
Is everything too hard for me?

softly they touch the depth of me,
can this be real someone that makes Jesus's death the reason to be
free.

When they are burnt out, he allows them to rest,
He allows them to vent so that they can be at their best.

you ever wonder why he cares so much,
he makes sure that there isn't one soul he hasn't touched.

When the body hurts, he removes the pain,
he says, "hey son, hey daughter you are not going insane."

Psalms Of A Prophet

Subtitle: In The Midst of It All I got an Answer

I made the two one so that they would be led by me,
They have experienced some rough patches in their life, but they
have the victory.

Even when they were caught up in life's little affairs,
He let them know to cast all their cares on him for he cares.

He makes them laugh at the very thought of him,
They have gotten very close even when their life was on a limb.

He knows how fragile they are, he never leaves them,
He keeps me in the palm of his hand, he would never let you be
stuck behind bars.

There are days they just want to be a baby,
He allows them to be that for a day and calls him daddy.

There are days when the nights seem so dark,
but he steps in and it's like heaven in an open park.

What made me fall in love with him was that the way he touched
them,
and for that, he and I will always be soul mates, that's why I am
healed, I just needed to touch his hem.

When at last the two shall become one after my own heart,
I will always protect my children from every fiery dart.

 A double fold blessing fall on them right now in every way,
that in season and out of season I'll be their fire by night and their
pillar of cloud by day.

Psalms Of A Prophet

Subtitle: In The Midst of It All I got an Answer

Smile and wipe the tears from your eyes for your work was not in
vain,
for I am God and I appreciate you staying in your lane.

Rejoice for your harvest is overflowing with good stock,
plant what you want but don't forget to feed my flock.

Lift up your head and walk with pride,
 for today your daddy takes you in his arms and walk right with you
side by side.

Unconditional

When was the last time I cried,
When was the last time tried?

As I listen to my heart beat strong,
I continue to ask myself, "Lord how long."

Over and over, I wonder what it is about me,
I see nothing, but Lord what do you see?

Psalms Of A Prophet

Subtitle: In The Midst of It All I got an Answer

What is it like to be loved all the time?
I don't know, I just sit taking things like a mime.

Lord I can't believe the hell I've been through,
Still is there anything for me to do?

I looked up with a shattered broken heart,
Each person has taken my heart apart.

Nevertheless, I'm a strong-willed man,
And I know there is a greater plan.

I've found a love that is greater than all,
It's called unconditional that can never fall.

Unexpected Events Take Heed - 8/2/20

Psalms Of A Prophet

Subtitle: In The Midst of It All I got an Answer

As I am laying in the bed, I can feel a shadow hovering over me,
The pressures of life spoke I come to break thee.

I began to call out to God what would you like for me to do?
God says this job is beyond what you would expect it will cost you
to give up you.

You see the ones that have professed me Lord over their life,
they no longer worship me they have brought me to dead sacrifice.

I am crying thinking in my mind have I did the same thing too,
The father speaks to me and says gather my room that I need you to
be the cleanup crew.

For you see my hands have always been on you since you were a
thought in my mind,
but the trumpets are about to sound off and the people are running
out of time.

I get off the bed with these assignments to carry out,
who will listen or will they say what's this all about?

I journeyed out and a church was the first stop I made,
oh, that this is the first but as I got close it was a stench that I wanted
to trade.

I'm crying because what used to have an aroma of God's fragrance is
no longer there,
the people have polluted it with so much sin in the air,
I got closer and a handwriting appeared, my presence is no longer
here.

Psalms Of A Prophet

Subtitle: In The Midst of It All I got an Answer

Grabbing my heart, the Imps of the enemy shows up and say we've
got to get this one from around this place,
I walked up to the enemy and said, "I rebuke you from time and
space you will no longer hold this place."

They realized they could no longer hold these people in shackles and
in chains,
time has been redeemed for them and God has released them from
their pain.

Leaving this church, I walked down further, and I came to this house
that was beautiful on the other side, but something was not right on
the inside,
I just there listening to what sounds like a lot lies, lies, lies.

Start hearing screams of stop hitting me and you're hurting me!
Kids are crying and neighbors ignoring the great tragedy.

I get closer to the door and imp comes to me and say we reside here,
you can no longer rest here at this place for God has heard their
tears,
and now I rebuke you and counsel the spirit of fear.

The spirit of peace now invades the place and this home,
What was broken is no longer functioning on its own,
the God I serve has just changed this tone.

I'm starting to realize that God needed someone to speak life,
These places have been abandoned by the ones that could shut down
the enemy's device.

God says return unto me you have lost your first love,

Psalms Of A Prophet

Subtitle: In The Midst of It All I got an Answer

I want to enrich your spirit and ascend you as a dove.

I am calling your spirit to hear me and this season for time is winding up,
Don't be caught sitting there empty, like a table spread it with an empty cup.

Take notice to what is around you,
gatekeepers wake up for there is an intruder around you,
I need you my sons and my daughters the time is now,
Take back the land and I will give you the town.

I am coming back sooner than you think,
don't be like a ship without a sail because you will surely sink,
Because I the father will appear before you can even blink.

WAIT A WHILE

WIND STARTS TO BLOW AND I WAIT,

TEARS ARE ROWING DOWN MY FACE PATIENTLY WAITING TO RELEASE MY FAITH.

I'M SEARCHING FOR AN ANSWER THAT WILL COMFORT ME,

SEEMS THEY ARE TRYING TO GAIN SOMETHING INSTEAD OF SEEING WHAT I SEE.

THE DOOR BEGAN TO CLOSE ON MY HEART FROM HURT,

WHILE THE REST OF THE PAIN INSIDE HELP ME STAY ALERT.

Psalms Of A Prophet

Subtitle: In The Midst of It All I got an Answer

WHAT IS IT THAT PEOPLE ARE TRYING TO GAIN,

IN THE PROCESS SAYING THE WRONG AND CAUSING A LOT
OF PAIN.

MY YEAR OF HAPPINESS IS COMING MY WAY,

THE BLESSINGS OF GOD WILL BEGAN TO SHOWER ME TODAY.

MY TEARS REPRESENT HOPE. JOY, LOVE, AND PEACE,

MY SMILE REPRESENTS LIFE EVERLASTING.

A CHILD CRIES OUT FOR HELP HOPING THAT SOMEONE WILL
HEAR,

JESUS CAME ALONG AND WIPED AWAY HIS TEARS.

WE SIT AND WONDER WHY MUST WE WAIT SO LONG,

FOR IF WE WNDURETH THE MORE WE BECOME STRONG.

WAIT I SAY JUST A LITTLE WHILE,

BECAUSE WEEPING MAY ENDURE FOR A NIGHT BUT GOD
WILL GIVE YOU A SMILE.

Psalms Of A Prophet

Subtitle: In The Midst of It All I got an Answer

Were You There?

When I was being talked about were you around?
No, you were part of the plan, that's what I found.

When I was being lied on in front of everyone did you stop it?
No, you were the main initiator surrounding the hit.

When I was crying in a bed of sorrow were you there to wipe my tears away?
No, you laughed at me and said have a nice day.

When my heart was aching from the pain, were you there to pray?
No, you added to the cause and yet you have so much to say.

When I was down and out were you there to help me?
No, you carried on like you were so high in God that you crucified me you see.

When I fell in a depression mode, were you there to encourage me?
No, you said I was good for nothing but to be trodden under the feet of men with no peace.

Now where were you when God deliver me from all of that?
Oh, you were outside gossiping talking about me behind my back.

Where were you when God use me to sing his word to a dying generation?
Oh, you were sipping and dipping having a good ole celebration.

Now that I've learned how to suffer and live right,
All the hell you put me through, where is your soul tonight?

You were so concern about what other people was doing you were not able to see the beams in your eyes,
But let you tell it; you were the anointed child the only one chosen to survive.

Now that you are in the old shape I use to be in,
Here is my hand for you to hold for all have sinned.

Psalms Of A Prophet

Subtitle: In The Midst of It All I got an Answer

I don't mind helping you out that's the spirit God gave to me,
So, I can help you gain the victory.

Now that I am free, feel free to call upon me at any time,
What I do for you is between you and I and I'll say nothing like a mime.

Now that you have learned to be there for others,
Don't stop, just stay humble and let God lead you to the sisters and brothers.

What About You 4/21/13

Follow me as I follow Christ so you can be saved,
or are you following me because you chose to be a slave?

I want you to live and be free,
not looking to seek after the things of royalty.

I saw you from afar off and there was something about you,
Until I got close, I realized you were sad and blue.

You were drawn to me because the love I carry inside,
not for you to cause me to attempt suicide.

I can only do what's in my ability,
not relying on my inner enemy.

I seek to destroy the very character of you,
yes, I saw what God was going to do.

I had to try to stop your destiny,
because the hedge around you I couldn't put my hands on thee.

God told me to seek you out,
He knew you would stand and have no doubt.

Psalms Of A Prophet
Subtitle: In The Midst of It All I got an Answer

You fail sometimes and I thought I had you,
but you repented, got up and you made it through.

I tried you with different tactics to cause you to go back,
you stood square your shoulders and said I will not fall off track.

I tried attacking your mind to have you bound up,
but you shocked me when you said Lord hears my broken cup.

I snatched your kids and caused them to go astray,
but you said for God I live and for God I will stay.

What is so special about this little OU,
because God said before I formed you, I knew you.

He must have a plan for your life,
He does so step back he already paid the price!

So, follow me as I follow Christ to the cross,
not stay damaged, broken, and your love like frost.

Where and Who I Am

Standing there me a room so cold, hello is anyone there?
Not an answer just a cold stare.

I'm looking at the mirror of my reflection hoping for
answer back,
Knowing that it is me with the power, did I fall off track?

But wait I see another image that overshadows me,
Not to worry or feast for it came to comfort me you see.

Psalms Of A Prophet

Subtitle: In The Midst of It All I got an Answer

I felt at peace with myself and who I was inside,
Not a one to destroy what was getting ready to show up on
the outside.

To know that I am loved by the one who created me,
For it was him gave me the victory.

They are whispering can you hear them calling your name,
I've blocked all of them that rise up against me for I'm not
ashamed.

Ripping away my identity to find out who I am,
Can they succeed, no, for I'm protected by the precious
lamb?

Do they stop lurking about?
No finding away because I 'm the one that stands out.

You come with your best shot, your charms, and your
sneaky ways,
But I'm a greater maneuver behind the wheel for there are
brighter days.

No more will you take me through the fire,
For I'm like an eagle I rise higher and higher,

So, take that little baler, you've just got fired!!

Where Art Thou? 8/18/13

The stench that is in my nostrils is not good,
And yet you say is it Me Lord or is it spoiled food?

You pretend that you love me day and night,
and yet I found in you that there's no light.

I'm tormented in my spirit because Adam where art thou?
Hiding behind the bushes telling you, my lullabies.

I canceled that off you so that I could use you,
and yet you return to the vomit and back to the voodoo.

You blame others for the sin in your own life,
Was it the people that caused you to pick up that knife?

You became self-righteous thinking that you are all of that,
always ready to jump on others like Chester the cat.

What happened to the times that we used to be intimate with each other,
oh, I realize you have change partners and took on a new lover.

I buried your sin in a consecrated ground,
now you're back cussing and fooling around.

Even when I gave you opportunity to get it right,

Psalms Of A Prophet

Subtitle: In The Midst of It All I got an Answer

You were too busy sleeping in the bed listening to Gladys Knight.

**I have not left you I am still here waiting on you,
let me show you the real love that I will bring you through.**

**Don't worry about what has happened in the past,
I said in my word, the last will be first and the first will be last.**

**I will take your sin and pardon your way,
you can smile I will cause your night to be turned into day.**

**I guarantee that there shall be no lack concerning you,
I celebrate you and I will cause others to wipe away the residue.**

**All things are passed away and all things become new,
Adam where art thou, let me love on you.**

Who Am I To You?

Sometimes through the storm I call you Peace,
But still, you ask who am I to you?

Sometimes through my trials I call you A WAY MAKER,
Even when the enemy wants to be a taker.

When the rain is pouring out hard and I can't see,
You step in and are my eyes for me.

Psalms Of A Prophet

Subtitle: In The Midst of It All I got an Answer

When the mountain becomes too high and they are in my way,
Father, you step in and say, "Be thou remove today!"

I chose you from birth out of your mother womb, I knew exactly
who you were to me,
A visionary to help set my people free.

Many nights you cried looking for me,
Yes, my son, I came to rescue thee.

You knew who I was from a young age,
But the enemy wanted to keep your mind in a cage.

My prince of peace in the midnight hour, that's who you are to me,
My daddy looked over my soul to see what I could not see.

When I was put on the back burner to always be last,
You step in Jesus and renew me with your holy gas.

You are the living word that lives way down in me,
To speak life to a dying world to be free in thee,
Lord that's who you are to me.

WHO HAS YOUR BACK?

Psalms Of A Prophet

Subtitle: In The Midst of It All I got an Answer

There is a battle that we must fight in order to survive,
If we give into it, we may not be revived.

I'd rather trust in God to work it out,
Instead of searching the world and standing in doubt.

How precious is my soul to my savior?
Not to those who are just there for their labor.

God gave me the keys to my future to choose the path that I wanted to walk,
But there are those that all they do is just talk.

All my fears and heartaches God said he will take care of,
And after that his spirit would ascend upon me as a dove.

I'm free, owe no one anything,
God made it that way so I could be something.

Yes, I must be ridicule for the path I chose to go down,
I must be talked about around the town.

I made the choice to go that way,
Now that God has given me joy this very day,
I am free to speak and say,
I knew nobody but God would make away.

I survive so can you!
There is nothing that God is not able to bring you through.

Trust him and don't doubt him for it is working for your good,
I know it seems hard when your mind is packed down like living in the hood.

Psalms Of A Prophet

Subtitle: In The Midst of It All I got an Answer

Nothing but grace will keep you from this mess,
That is the joy of the Lord and his kindness.

Know who you are and don't you doubt it for one bit God has your back,
Although it may get hard and you may fall off track,
Trust God no matter what; guess what he has your back.

Who Will Be My Voice

As he guides you to a place called, "PEACE",

With Jesus you can live to be free.

He calls us out into a place of praise,

Trying to keep your mind from going insane.

He blesses your life in different varieties,

But we take him for granted in different societies.

I called you to be a weapon of warfare,

Not live a life in complete despair.

Can I make it through this terrible storm?

Didn't I tell you I will protect you from all harm?

Psalms Of A Prophet

Subtitle: In The Midst of It All I got an Answer

Who am I to you, my child?

A balm in Gilead to help you through your trial.

I'm crying for my people, and they won't hear,

Come home to the father while he is near.

Dry your weeping eyes I hear your cry,

I see you on the banks of Jordan standing next in line.

My miracle is about to come through,

My child, my child, don't you know I love you.

My children are falling away from me,

Who will be my voice so they can walk in victory?

The word said they would turn away from the truth,

I called you to walk in Christianity that's what I told you.

Who will be my voice for a dying nation?

Will you let them perish because you thought you had a revelation?

Psalms Of A Prophet

Subtitle: In The Midst of It All I got an Answer

I cry cause of all of the strife,

Brothers and sisters at each other's throat with knives.

Who will be my voice for the sick and shut in,

Who will say, "Be healed and win".

I need a voice to say, "Hear am I use me".

Who will be the voice for my people to live eternally?

Speak life to dry bones and set my people free.

Psalms Of A Prophet

Subtitle: In The Midst of It All I got an Answer

You Are Strength – 5/4/20.

I was claiming this place of defeat never allowing my soul to be free,
looking for answers in different places not realizing the word was in me.

I expressed to others on the fear that I carried within me,
never realizing that I was becoming the biggest enemy.

I heard inside of me you are strength you can do this,
I was doing for everyone until the father touched me with a single kiss.

I found this strength that I've always had to continue in this walk,
Along the way I had some very interesting talks.

He takes me on this journey where the Lord shows me his heart,
Undeserving of what he gives to me he says no this I have set you apart.

Scared not wanting to be different from everyone else in this time,
He says I give you the words to stop standing there like a mime!

You were predestined to be used for my glory,
don't allow what's around you to affect your story.

I have given you strength to win this race,

Psalms Of A Prophet

Subtitle: In The Midst of It All I got an Answer

Don't go too fast pace yourself, your past the enemy can't even throw in your face.

When I thought of you, I thought of strength you would possess, I crafted you in my image so you could live life to the fullest.

I am strength a strength like no other, my love for you keeps taking you further and further.

Why do you doubt what you can do for me, I understand you are afraid of messing up, I've already seen it in your destiny.

It does not change the plans that I have towards you, Even when you are crying, feeling down and feeling blue my heart still says I love you.

I am strength when you are weak, I am the door and the life that you seek.

My child, hold your head up for you have caught my heart, My never-ending love for you will never ever depart.

Embrace the destiny that is on your life, for I the father sent my son to be the ultimate sacrifice.

I know you didn't understand the strength that you carried in you, many will come for you, and you will lead them out of Kalamazoo.

I will stand with you through this fight, but it's my spirit and not by your might.

Psalms Of A Prophet

Subtitle: In The Midst of It All I got an Answer

Trust me to handle the load that you will have to bear,
I will never leave you nor forsake you but the heavy load I will
share.

Wipe your eyes my child says the Lord of hosts,
for I am raising up a mighty remnant from the north, South, east, and
the West Coast.

They shall sound the alarm and the horns will blow,
You will know them by the direction of the way the wind flows.

Arise the trumpets are blowing tell my people to repent,
for the king has a table spread it but were all of you sent?

I am calling, is anyone listening to me?
Lead them to come for they shall have the true victory.

I will swallow up pride and consume the malicious ones,
I will deal with them that live by the sword and guns.

Oh, death where is your sting?
Oh, my children, where are the songs that you sing?
Or do you follow your own path and do your own thing?

Strength comes to you this day,
for you are my vessel I formed you from clay,
I say unto you I am the God that will make a way,
Do you trust me, hello, do you hear what I say?

Psalms Of A Prophet

Subtitle: In The Midst of It All I got an Answer

Your Desire but Not My Will 8-13-11

Can you hear me when I called,
can you not see that ditch you are getting ready to fall!

Why have you forsaken the one I sent to you,
You stabbed them not knowing I used them to be a blessing to you.

Psalms Of A Prophet

Subtitle: In The Midst of It All I got an Answer

You disagree with the one I sent,
How dare you abuse my child? It's time for you to repent!

You ask me for my fruits of my spirit so you can lead,
but you walk after the flesh and planting bad seeds.

You can no longer hear my children cry,
can I not find 50 standing on the front line?

You pick up trash along the way,
you decided to switch roles you become the Potter and made God the clay.

You can no longer distinguish between right and wrong,
you have disdained my name speaking with a fake tongue!

I am a way of escape for them that diligently seek me,
They will shine and walk with great integrity.

They are soldiers ready to fight the good fight,
They stay on their knees both day and night.

Your mouth is forever running keeping up mess,
fear not my child I will not have you in distress.

In three days, I rose up from the grave,
for you were bought with a price you are not a slave!

In three days, I will cause you to be swallowed up by a fish,
I will cause your life to be served to you on a dish.

Psalms Of A Prophet

Subtitle: In The Midst of It All I got an Answer

In this experience I am stripping away the fleshly desires,
you will walk in truth you will not be a liar!

To know me is to love me,
follow me as I follow the one that has set my destiny.

I called you to come out from among the wolves that pretended to be with you,
but at the given chance destroy the very character of you.

Remember who I am the almighty one,
The Great I Am is my name and all your battles will be won.

Psalms Of A Prophet

Subtitle: In The Midst of It All I got an Answer

Zachary Prayer 3-7-11

THEY ARE LIKE GLUE STUCK BY MY SIDE,
BUT IN MIDST OF PRAYER, I HEAR THE WORD SUICIDE.

AS I WENT DEEPER, DEATH BACKED OFF BECAUSE HE HAD
NO POWER,
I REMEMBER THAT GOD SAID, "I AM A STRONG TOWER."

BREATHED INTO ME OH LORD, I NEED THEE,
USE ME AS YOUR VESSEL SO THAT YOUR PEOPLE MIGHT BE
FREE.

YOU WILL BE HATED WITHOUT A CAUSE AND DECREE,
THEY ARE WATCHING YOUR CHARACTER AND WHAT'S IN
THEE.

Psalms Of A Prophet

Subtitle: In The Midst of It All I got an Answer

LOOK AT THE STORM AND SAY TO IT PEACE!
YOU CANNOT TAKE ME OUT, YOU WILL NOT STOP MY
INCREASE.

MY PRAYER IS JUST A CONCERN FOR WHAT IS GOING ON,
STAND UP, PACK YOUR BAG, GIRD YOURSELF FOR YOU ARE
BEING BROUGHT BEFORE THE THRONE.

WELCOME IN COME AND TAKE A SEAT RIGHT THERE BY MY
SAVIOR FEET FOR YOU MADE IT IN,
I KNEW YOU COULD ENDURE UNTIL THE END,
TODAY IS CELEBRATION TIME FOR YOU WIN, WIN, WIN.

Made in the USA
Middletown, DE
12 January 2024